M000040000

ADVANCE PRAISE FOR *CITIZEN TRUMP*

"Filmmaker Robert Orlando probes some of the secrets of Trump's obsessions, and finds answers in what the president has described as his favorite film… Striking, very watchable. Fascinating film!"

> —Michael Medved, Movie Critic

"Robert Orlando's 2020 documentary shows Trump's favorite film is a road map to his methods."

> —Joseph Serwach, Medium

"To do so, he tells President Trump's life story in the cinematographic style of *Citizen Kane*, incorporating the iconic snow globe, the campaign poster, and even the mysterious word ('Rosebud') that is central to Orson Welles' masterpiece."

> —Gabriel Andrade, *Merion West*

"Through the lens of the 1941 classic *Citizen Kane*, a documentary filmmaker seeks to understand the life journey of President Trump and his successful venture into politics."

—Josh Shepherd, *The Federalist*

"This is the fascinating parallel that inspired Robert Orlando. The film is remarkable—truly in the literal sense. It's visually engaging, if not riveting."

—Paul Kengor, *The American Spectator*

CITIZEN TRUMP

A ONE MAN SHOW

ROBERT ORLANDO

Post Hill
PRESS

A POST HILL PRESS BOOK
ISBN: 978-1-64293-916-3
ISBN (eBook): 978-1-64293-917-0

Citizen Trump:
A One Man Show
© 2021 by Robert Orlando
All Rights Reserved

Cover design by Jason Pearson, Nexus Media
llustrations by David Orlandelli, Nexus Media

No part of this book may be reproduced, stored in a retrieval system, or transmitted by any means without the written permission of the author and publisher.

Post Hill Press
New York • Nashville
posthillpress.com

Published in the United States of America

1 2 3 4 5 6 7 8 9 10

*I dedicate this book to the memory of
Orson Welles (1915–1985) and to anyone
who has suffered from the COVID-19 virus.*

TABLE OF CONTENTS

*Until you make the unconscious conscious,
it will direct your life and you will call it fate.*
—C. G. Jung

04

05

ALTERNATIVE SHOT
ORLANDO IN THE BALCONY

THE FILMMAKER'S JOURNEY

"A media virus seeks a host. One obvious media figure filled that role. Born to a family of great wealth. Started as a businessman and ran for political office. He would use his profile in media to reach his audience. He spoke with great hyperbole. He would run for office as a result of feeling slighted by his political opponents. His campaign ran on a populist message of America first. He would be accused of having supported white nationalists, and being engaged with dictators. In the end he would lose his campaign. Yes, of course, it was William Randolph Hearst. And his life provided the subject for what would become the greatest film ever made, Citizen Kane."—Robert Orlando

Donald Trump has dominated the media news cycle 24/7 for four years. Some days it feels like forty years. At the time, you can look in any direction, on any screen, and see Trump. I had competed with his media omnipresence during the production and release of two of my earlier films, *Silence Patton* and *The Divine Plan*. Even so, development of a project about Trump has long been on my mind. But how to tell a story that has been told so many times and in so many ways?

Oddly enough, I found my answer in the middle of a pandemic. When COVID-19 hit, it had me locked in my studio without work and worrying if I had the disease. To pass the time, I rewatched some of my favorite films, culminating with the American black-and-white classic *Citizen Kane*. In the context of 2020 and in the midst of the virus and a contentious election, I was struck by the similarities between the film's protagonist, Charles Foster Kane, and our own modern-day Citizen Trump. Then and there I found the way into my film: examine Trump through the lens of Kane. When I discovered that *Citizen Kane* was Trump's favorite film, I had my title! It was time to roll the camera.

A Character Study

Though Trump was in the throes of campaigning for a second term, my aim was *not* to produce a political film. As an independent filmmaker, I was more interested in pursuing a deep character study into one of the most controversial figures of our time. My template was not a Right vs. Left, faith vs. nonfaith, or even madness vs. sanity paradigm, but to explore the archetypes of storytelling as expressions of interior character, especially where Trump and Kane were so amazingly similar.

Like most New Yorkers, my perception of Trump had been that of a gossip column showman seeking media attention. To some degree, I just accepted him as is: the man who built Trump

Tower, his latest affair, his special TV appearances—you name it. He added a charm to the NY landscape as far back as Rona Barrett's show, where she asked him if he'd like to be the president of the United States.[1] Or later in his friendly repartee on David Letterman. You would read about him in the *New York Post* one day or hear him on Howard Stern the next, but he was rarely seen as a threat. Many of us just assumed even his best real estate deals were partly shady, though I never bothered to dig into the details back then.

Periodically, Trump would announce a run for president, usually as a publicity stunt to sell books. But he would bail out once his books were bestsellers. Of course, he made good on one of those runs, and it was then, several years into his presidency that my idea for *Citizen Trump* took shape. COVID-19 had created a somber mood in which to conjure my vision: What if, at the center of a deadly global pandemic, it fell to a fast-talking showman to lead America out of danger? Pre-COVID, as the stock market boomed, many people overlooked Trump's excesses, content to ride the prosperity wave. But as the disease ran rampant, it put the performer on the defensive. The urgent questions

---

1   NewsChannel 3-12. "EXCLUSIVE: Rona Barrett Reflects on 1980 Interview with Then-Developer Donald Trump." NewsChannel 3-12, November 7, 2017. Web.

became: Did Trump have the ability to switch roles and play the transparent leader, to be knowledgeable, direct, and reassuring? How would he deal with a crisis that not only could destroy the lives of hundreds of thousands but also wipe out his presidency?

Producer/director Orson Welles asked a similar question when exploring the formidable William Randolph Hearst, the model for his main character in *Citizen Kane*. Like Trump, Kane was a man of acquisitions, a media tycoon who ran for office, then suffered a great fall. Would Citizen Trump suffer the same fate? Could the parallels in their lives predict the outcome for Trump?

My fascination with Kane began in film school when I first felt the power of sound, light, and action in the hands of a master. Welles—to me—was a titan, all four faces of cinema's Mount Rushmore: actor, producer, writer, and director. He was also a theater and radio star. Coincidentally, my studio was located across from Princeton University and the next town over from Hopewell, New Jersey, where Welles located his legendary *War of the Worlds* broadcast in 1938.

That broadcast was an unforgettable moment in radio history. Welles's voice transfixed his audience, convincing many the world was experiencing an alien attack. With war already spreading across Europe, invasion was on the public's mind, much as the news about the invasion and spread of COVID has been on our collective minds. As we sheltered in place, streets emptied, and stores and restaurants closed, I remained in a quiet old brick building. That's when I switched on the old movies to shut out the medical news, the election, and Trump. Or at least tried to.

I found that blocking out the relentless media noise was key to opening a whole new perspective. For a short while, COVID allowed us to return to a simpler time. Refreshing, really, because the way we engage our world has left us precious little opportunity to be still, to quietly process ideas, to think. We're assaulted by nonstop data through our phones, cable news, memes, Twitter, Facebook, and an onslaught of social media platforms. And since 2016, the war between the media and Trump has been a daily dose of vitriol. It has been the grand narrative of our times and an unavoidable topic if one wants to remain relevant. In my self-imposed COVID prison, I concluded it was time for me to make my statement about the Man and the Times, and *Citizen Kane* would be my vehicle.

My pick for best film of all time goes to *Citizen Kane*, a seamless visual masterpiece and a technical inspiration. In this one film, Welles introduced myriad innovations, breaking form and storytelling in new ways. It was incomparable at the time, almost docudrama in style. His pre-Hollywood background fed his achievement. He had an ear for radio and knew that the simplest sounds—a clock ticking, a distant dog barking, the wind—can transform a sequence. From his years in theater, he understood the effectiveness of proper stage blocking. In *Kane*, the camera moves through the noir-esque world as an objective bystander, the actors stepping in and out of the frame.

Orson Welles, the man, provided me with further inspiration. His life bore an uncanny resemblance to the character Kane. The film is a work of genius and also a cautionary tale. I hold mixed thoughts about Welles and the Kane phenomenon. On one hand, he was the mercurial boy wonder with the "largest train set" ever in Hollywood, but his early fame (achieved in part by poking at Hearst) and a lack of discipline almost ended his creative and personal life. Only this once was Welles able to exercise his talents without restraint. Welles often said he "started at the top and worked his way down." For most of his career, he could not make a living in Tinseltown.

As I say in my film, and without judgment, there is a lot of Kane in Orson Welles. Likewise, there is probably some of Trump in me. Could there be another lens through which we can view and therefore explain and find meaning in the rise of

Trump? Something beyond him that he may be unaware of or only partly aware of?

Trump as Antihero

Trump, like Kane, is an antihero, in that his blind spots and flaws are self-wounding; however, in spite of his flaws, Trump surpassed Kane's failed run for governor to become president of the United States. As I thought more about film and about Trump himself, it became clear that Trump emerged as a consequence of the Obama presidency, an administration that dismissed traditional Americans, reducing them to crazy, religious gun owners. In this conflict, Obama was the antagonist, with a posse that included Hilary Clinton and the media. Media in general, but CNN and MSNBC in particular, was berating Trump. Fox was his champion, and for four years that was our ongoing reality TV.

And what of Trump? The reality star as president had not helped himself by using daily briefings for self-promotion or taking frequent trips to Mar-a-Lago, which is reminiscent of Kane's own private fortress, Xanadu. As I pondered the similarities, it occurred to me that, whether it's Trump or the fictional Kane, the media's white noise is the same. In the old days not so long ago, one might step into a darkened theater to escape that small screen noise for an intimate story. My dark studio became my theater, only to find myself watching the same story I had seen on the small screen, on the big screen.

The parallels of Kane and Trump had been remarked on, but suddenly they were clear to see. Kane, with all his power and self-aggrandizement, forgot something essential and sacred: he forgot the necessity for genuine human connection. This ultimately left him alone, sad, and tragic. Too late, Kane would recognize what he had let slip through his fingers—his "Rosebud" moment. In the case of Trump, after his loss in the 2020 election, he too would isolate himself in the White House, except for a few loyalists—though we have not seen the "end of the movie" and can only speculate what might be his Rosebud moment. We all have them. Those places and moments when we look back at the unresolved bits of our own past. Without that gaze backward, there is no looking forward. Could Kane's too-late discovery offer a road map to the next chapter in the Trump narrative?

So, as I considered the elements of this project, there was me as the storyteller, the subjects Kane and Trump, the ghost of Welles, and then, of course, the audience. It's the audience that is my real concern. I was determined to look past the projected images of Trump as defined by the politicians and the news, and like an old-time filmmaker, peer into the faces of the viewers and readers. After all, we all need a respite, like an old matinee in the middle of a workday (for those old enough to recall them). Outside the theater real life goes on. Whether in the aftermath of this latest election or the next one in four years, the course our country is on is not predetermined. One person's performance in media should not be the criteria for our choice of leaders. Reality TV is as much about us as it is about the performers. Kane kept resonating in my head as I considered my main character.

The Stage Is the Thing

So, as Trump took center stage in my film, I set out to discover the motivations and seeming success of his pre-presidential career. How did this unlikely candidate capture the imagination of voters who hailed his arrival? Many believe that a radical voice had been reshaping and even erasing our traditions and historic legacy. Call it political correctness or cultural warfare, nearly half of the population was left feeling desperate for a leader who could halt the progressive agenda, a gunslinger and take-no-prisoners trailblazer. Enter Donald Trump—a self-sufficient, self-described billionaire with a successful reality TV show and *big* personality. He was a practiced showman, equipped to match the effect of 24/7 media, a slate of other Republican candidates, and the Democratic machine and not just survive, but win!

Most voters knew Trump was morally flawed but didn't really care. By 2016, their stake in a national identity was worth more than the requirement that Trump wear a white hat. To his base, Trump was (and remains) the antidote, or "chemotherapy," to a media that has overstepped its role. He was a levee against a tide of change. People felt Trump might have been the only figure standing between the America they knew and the America to be erased. Like Kane, he became, at least in public, the champion of the forgotten people.

Welles wanted to call out Kane (Hearst) and his obsession with acquisitions that were much more numerous and grandiose than even Trump's—a drive that places material gain and human excess above the human bonds of virtue. On some level, Welles was speaking to himself, as I am likely writing to myself about Trump. There was a part of himself that Welles did not want to lose completely, a part that was damaged from having been abandoned, working as a child star, and acting as caretaker to his alcoholic father. And we have come to learn that Trump's childhood was far from ideal. My identification with Trump is likely in his ambition, as one who sees the value of being in the spotlight, of needing a stage. After all, you can't share a good story if no one is listening. You can't make a high-production-value show without a big budget.

And being a blind believer in yourself, if not to a fault, doesn't hurt. Trump was from Queens. I was from Brooklyn and had moved into Manhattan before making my own journey out to Hollywood. And for all the ambition and drive and glitz, there is a dark side, or as Carl Jung would call it, a shadow side. In Citizen Trump we don't know how these inner demons will play out after one term as president, but we know there is a shadow side to all success, a loss and gain, a "Rosebud."

Citizen Kane is all-too-human a story. It is about the rise and fall of the powerful, the archetype of the father figure or moral king, and it is rare when they do not fall. They fall not because they are in a political struggle but because they lose awareness of their own corruptibility. It's the same for Trump, but added to his archetype is the leader as trickster (or shapeshifter), one who can hold an audience without restriction. I wanted to capture that in this book, not only for those in my age group but with millennials in mind, those who do not have the length of life to see the patterns of those who come and go, rise and fall. What I want to tell them is to be like Welles, bold and independent-minded. Forget the herd and find your own voice. And for God's sake, watch the great films, the stories that tell us so much about ourselves and the hero's journey.

Thank God for movies.

ORLAN
HOLDIN
THE
SNOWGLO

THEN
SHAKIIN
THE
GLOB

ORLAN
PUTTING
THE GL
DOWN

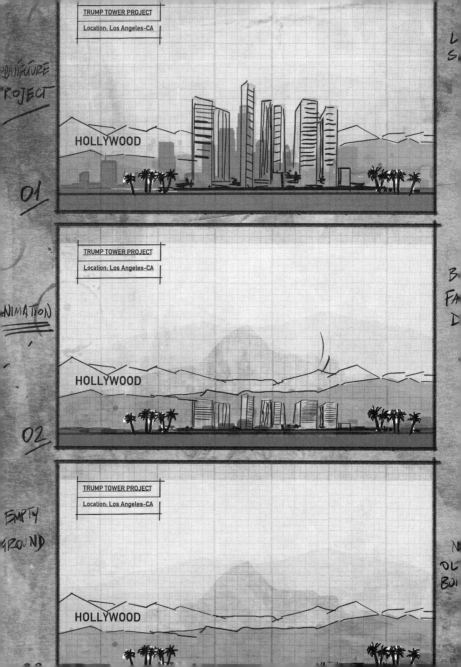

1. ROLL CAMERA

Rosebud...
—Kane

For decades, film critics have lauded *Citizen Kane* as one of the most important films in American cinema. Orson Welles wrote, directed, and starred in the 1941 classic. Although Welles claimed his protagonist, Charles Foster Kane, was an amalgam of characters, most knew his target was William Randolph Hearst. My own fascination with Donald Trump mirrors that of Welles'. I continue to find the similarities between Trump and Kane uncanny. Here, for example, is an observation about the fictional Kane that could easily describe Trump: "His acquaintances . . . credit him with personal charm, but do not deny his ruthlessness in business operations. Shopkeepers and his nearest rivals are simply not in his class. Here is success on a dizzying and truly American scale."[2]

Welles, as a world-class showman himself, knew he had to make the film relevant, as he had with his onstage Black *Macbeth*

---

2   Charles River Editors. *William Randolph Hearst, Orson Welles, and Citizen Kane: The History of the Men behind One of America's Most Famous Movies*. Ann Arbor, MI: Charles River Editors, 2019. p. 1.

in Harlem and his radio stunt, *War of the Worlds.* The *New York Tribune* columnist Dorothy Thompson acclaimed the broadcast "one of the most fascinating and important events of all time . . . he made the scare to end all scares, the menace to end all menaces."[3] It was a seismic theatrical event and a sign to come of the power of media.

So, when Welles hit Hollywood as a first-time film director, he understood that he had to create buzz, which he did by rattling the cage of the powerful Hearst. What he couldn't have known was that nearly eighty years later, another formidable man, Donald Trump, would take his cues from *Citizen Kane*. Welles, through the skill of his storytelling, uncovered deep truths and exposed character. Welles understood films as the looking glass for how we understand ourselves. "It is a curious fact that whenever Welles spoke of films that he admired, he cited the great neo-realists: Rossellini, DeSica, and so on," writes Simon Callow in *Orson Welles, Volume 1: The Road to Xanadu*. Callow adds, "Their warmth, richness and sense of life lived transcended, he said, any technical limitations."

Welles opens the film with Kane whispering the most chilling and iconic word in Hollywood history: "Rosebud." As the

---

3   Callow, Simon. *Orson Welles, Volume 1: The Road to Xanadu*. New York, NY: Viking, 1996. p. 415.

camera enters the shadows, the audience sees the main character take his final breath as he releases a snow globe that crashes to the floor. The singular word lures us into a private moment of tragedy. Trump, the American audience, and this filmmaker have for decades been spellbound.

After digging deep into this project, I discovered that some news coverage and even biographers believe Trump might have based his own life and fortune on Kane. Sound a little far-fetched? Well, it would not be the first time someone was inspired by a film. At first, I was skeptical, but now . . . well, maybe the best answer is to keep reading!

Like Kane, Trump aspired to greatness. Both crafted public facades to mask private insecurities. Each made themselves larger than life. And each was empowered by early failures. In our story, however, we begin with a lesser-known Trump, a man initially driven to become a movie mogul. He wanted to be a star. He has said: "I was attracted to the glamour of the movies, and I admired guys like Sam Goldwyn, Darryl Zanuck, and most of all Louis B. Mayer, whom I considered great showmen. But in the end I decided real estate was a much better business."[4] When his

4   Poniewozik, James. *Audience of One: Donald Trump, Television, and the Fracturing of America*. New York, NY: Liveright Publishing Corporation, 2019. p. 13.

Hollywood dreams failed, he tried on a new role as New York real estate tycoon.

As author of *Audience of One*, James Poniewozik states plainly, "So no film school. Fordham University. Transfer to Wharton. Back to New York, back to dad's office." Once Hollywood was out, Trump carried the acting bug across career lines. Perhaps without the needed skills to play featured characters on the silver screen, Trump's better option was to play himself as a star. In this sense the formula for his reality TV personality was always one in the making.

Trump's hybrid of Hollywood, New York real estate, business, and eventually politics was rehearsed over twenty-five years. Katie Couric, when interviewed for the book *The Method to the Madness,* stated, "If the city is a play, then he's a character in that city, a Damon Runyon-type guy. He was never really embraced by New York society or the big swinging you-know-whats of Wall Street. He never had the street cred that he was searching for or got the imprimatur of some of those more sophisticated social people, and it drove him crazy . . . He definitely knew how to write a tabloid story. He just had a natural ability to communicate in bold headlines . . . His persona was beginning to take shape."[5]

5   Salkin, Allen, and Aaron Short, *The Method to The Madness*. New York, NY: All Points, 2019. p. 15.

The Trump Story

Trump realized early that stories need a beginning, a middle, and an end. Conflict is also key. Whether told on the silver screen, reality TV, or the political stage, stories need a villain, a victim, and a hero. Robert McKee in his well-known film industry work on screenwriting states the Principle of Antagonism: "A protagonist and his story can only be intellectually fascinating and emotionally compelling as the forces of antagonism make them."[6] The hero and the villain do battle, usually competing for the same prize: fame, power, sex. In the case of Trump, the conflict would escalate to the level of warfare. As author Poniewozik puts it, "Trump . . . believed, like a born reality-TV producer, that warfare and distrust were the most productive and entertaining modes of existence."[7] Both Trump and Kane knew how to start a war.

In the case of the antihero, the lines between the good and the bad (and occasionally the ugly) are not so obvious. Antiheroes are not morally upstanding, but they can still look like good guys compared to an even worse villain. And herein lies the grand strategy: a triangulation of mortal combat with a villain and victim and a hero, a formulation as old as stories them-

---

6   McKee, Robert. *Story*. New York, NY: HarperCollins, 1997. p. 317.
7   Poniewozik, *Audience of One*, p. 135.

selves. Whether in Greek tragedy or the modern Western or war film, antiheroes have always been part of the repertoire. In Victor Davis Hanson's book *A Case for Trump*, he explains that tragic heroes and antiheroes are often unlikable. Sophocles' Oedipus in "Oedipus Rex" was rudely narcissistic. In the film *Hombre*, John Russell (Paul Newman) proved arrogant and off-putting. Achilles in Homer's *Iliad* is self-absorbed and pouts that his service is never rewarded. Does this sound familiar?[8]

Trump is the antihero brought up to date for reality TV. Early on, he took calculated steps to look the part. He rewrote his privileged but unglamorous beginnings. Like Kane, Trump adopted the persona of a self-made man. Never mind that both characters had been handed a substantial inheritance—in Trump's case, $15 million, which he invested (with some questionable behavior) in a Manhattan hotel.

Next, Trump invested in the creation of great enemies. As he stepped into the role of political antihero, Trump squared off against what he had defined as the enemies of America: the evil media, the swampy establishment, and China. But he was not paving new ground; he was reading the media and extracting what he needed from some influential fictional characters in

8   Hanson, Victor Davis. *The Case for Trump*. New York, NY: Basic Books, 2020. p. 317.

addition to Kane. As Poniewozik reminds us, his "psyche was formed by television. . . . The exploits of ruthless, charismatic men (with a few exceptions, it was largely men) occupied *The Sopranos, Deadwood*, and *Breaking Bad.*"[9] Later in Trump's presidency, Steve Bannon would say to the *New York Times*, "Dude, he's Archie Bunker." He meant it as a compliment.[10]

With the ground softened by TV antiheroes, he could begin his land attack and fashion himself into the champion and protector of Middle America. Wielding his signature catchphrase, Make America Great Again (MAGA), Trump transformed from tabloid curiosity to presidential candidate. As Poniewozik points out, the MAGA slogan "was neither rosy optimism nor gloom-and-doom decline. Instead, it came off to half the country as can-do-ism."

Trump leveraged his antihero persona on social media, cable news, and television to launch himself into the White House. And yet, it is at the peak of accomplishment—as it was with Kane—that cracks begin to show and where a character's destiny is once again proved. With Trump in the Oval Office, Americans discover what it is like to live inside a reality TV show programmed for conflict, entertainment, and self-adulation. It is a

9   Poniewozik, *Audience of One*, p. 88.
10   Ibid, p. 88–91.

phenomenon that the modern audience might find new and excit-
ing but in truth is ancient. Hanson writes that the 5th century BC
comic dramatist Aristophanes, "in right wing populist fashion,
had ridiculed Athenian gentry and its subsidized followers."[11]

Given the similarities of past with present, is it any surprise that some of our classic movie characters like Citizen Kane
would emerge in our Citizen Trump? Let's journey to explore—
and possibly even understand—the forty-fifth president. What
do Kane and Trump have in common? Why would one win and
the other lose in their attempts at high office? How did Trump, a
failed businessman with an unceasing desire for media attention
and no political experience, prepare to play the role of a lifetime?

The Role of Presidency

Studying a U.S. president through the lens of film and television
might seem a trivializing exercise. Yet, when asked how his acting career served him in the role of president, Ronald Reagan
responded that he didn't know how he could have been president
without that training. John Kennedy defeated Richard Nixon in
a televised debate largely because his opponent refused to wear
makeup. Even Franklin Roosevelt, in conversation with Orson

---

11   Hanson, *The Case for Trump*, p. 18.

Welles, recognized the magic of film, suggesting they were the two greatest actors in the world.

Our ears and eyes and noses process the symbolic behavior of those who stand in front of the throngs, and we still believe they know something we do not. They might. In any case, they are playing their roles for us, and that much they know with metaphysical certitude.

Film and television help us explore and understand the archetypes of personality, what Swiss psychologist Carl Jung would describe as persona. Through film, we recognize stereotypes like the bully or the damsel in distress, the trickster or the outlaw. Trump reveals his admiration for Jung's theories on persona in his book *How to Get Rich*. Masks are our persona, and they provide a way to perform in the world. We have a public mask and a private mask. Yet Trump was quick to recognize that a man can lose himself behind the mask if he's not careful. He cautioned, "Just don't become your persona."

Too much persona can release what Jung described as the shadow, or the dark side, of personality, the pure impulse toward power, fame, and pleasure without concern for consequence. In *Citizen Kane*, audiences are witness to the shadow as it slowly haunts then overtakes the fallen man. Could this masterpiece, which plumbs the psychological depths and motivations of a fictional media tycoon, help explain the motives, aspirations, and insecurities of America's president?

As with the fictional Kane, many of Trump's early attempts at grandeur came up short. He engaged in a series of shady real estate deals and a few symbolic wins like rescuing the Central Park skating rink. Trump made his name at the famed Kit Kat Club, buying drinks for models and exaggerating his net worth (an ongoing pattern). Investigative journalist and author David Cay Johnston writes, "In 1990, when his business empire was on the verge of collapse, Trump told me and many other journalists that he was worth $3 billion. He told others $5 billion. I got my hands on a copy of his personal net worth statement that spring, which revealed a much smaller figure. Two months later, a report commissioned by his bankers and introduced in regulatory hearings put Trump in the red by almost $300 million."[12] This was three decades before the *New York Times* report on his tax returns.

In another revealing anecdote, Trump made a call to a *Forbes* reporter under his favorite fictitious name, John Barron. "Barron" tried to convince the journalist he should rank higher

---

12   Johnston, David Cay. *The Making of Donald Trump*. Brooklyn, NY: Melville House Publishing, 2017. p. 77.

on the prestigious Forbes 400 list. And David Cay Johnston tells this story: "After the destruction of the Bonwit Teller building to build Trump Tower, a chorus of New Yorkers criticized Trump's decision to destroy the facade art along with it. A front-page *New York Times* story reported unsuccessful attempts to reach Trump. Instead, the paper got a call from John Barron, a vice president of the Trump Organization. He said that taking down the sculptures would have cost $32,000, delayed the construction of Trump Tower by three weeks, and run the risk of killing people if the stones crashed to the ground.[13] Johnston describes this 1991 response when Trump used a second pseudonym: "The caller identified himself as John Miller. He said he had just been hired to handle Donald Trump's public relations because The Donald was too busy to return calls himself, given the 'important, beautiful women who call him all the time.'"[14] Donald would add, "You know, it really doesn't matter what [the media] write as long as you've got a young and beautiful piece of ass."

---

13   Ibid., p. 135.

14   Ibid., p. 140. On that same call, Trump went on that Miller told Carswell that Carla Bruni (Donald's girlfriend) had a fling with guitarist Eric Clapton before starting "a big thing" with Mick Jagger, "and then she dropped Mick Jagger for Donald, and that's where it is right now. And again he's not making any commitments to Carla, just so you understand."

While Trump's tactics might be decried by many, a few have come to appreciate his directness and media savvy. One-time friend, advertising guru, and CNBC host Donny Deutsch claims you can "call him an idiot savant, whatever you want, but I've never seen a guy who understands messaging and consistency of messaging and staying on brand and being able to be true to the brand but also evolve the brand at the same time. The guy's a genius."[15] The same could be said of the newspaper mogul Kane who knew how to maintain distinction and hold the country's attention with his own brand of yellow journalism.

Part of Trump's genius would be the self-advocacy (though fictional) of his success and sexual prowess. As John Miller, he promoted his playboy status after breaking up with Marla Maples, claiming among other things that he (Trump) "has a lot of options, and frankly gets called by everybody." He would also place in Maples' mouth the admission that he was the best sex she ever had.[16] He was a master of it all. It's all about getting out there, keeping your name in the paper, and changing direction and changing the subject, keeping people hanging on.[17]

---

15   Salkin and Short, *Method to the Madness,* p. 22.

16   Brooke, Jill. "The Real Story Behind Donald Trump's Infamous 'Best Sex I've Ever Had' Headline (Guest Column)." *The Hollywood Reporter.* April 12, 2018. Web.

17   Salkin and Short, *Method to the Madness,* p. 13.

There was similar embellishment in the later world of ac-quisitions and casinos. Even buying Mar-a-Lago, Marjorie Mer-riweather Post's grand Palm Beach folly, was not exactly the tri-umph of a super-successful businessman. Three potential sales collapsed before Donald Trump bought the property in 1985. He paid a reported $8 million for the estate and its furnishings—a small fraction of the original cost, no matter how you calculate it. That sale went through, but little known is that Trump burned through his early inheritance and racked up ill-will among inves-tors. He took out, then defaulted on, a $245 million loan to buy an airline. Other ventures—everything from beverages, board games, magazines, mortgages, and steaks—also resulted in de-fault or bankruptcy. Newspapers accused him of consorting with mobsters like Paul Castellano and Tony Salerno and using his helicopter to fly them around. His biggest gamble and eventual failure came with his foray into Atlantic City casinos. After big-time live events and dates with the stars such as Mike Tyson and Don King, poor management and shady dealings left him a debt hostage to Deutsche Bank. He ended in bankruptcy and divorce court. He had exhausted even the support of his father through a lifetime of high-stakes gambling and excess. At the nadir of his early journey, he was governed by the banks, keeping him as

Too Big to Fail.[18] Put another way, "Citibank needed him to keep playing his character."[19] Was it his character role as a high-stakes gambler that led him to the financial abyss? At the time, early biographer Wayne Barrett writes in his introduction that Donald Trump's press agent tried to "persuade me to delete the use of the word 'downfall' in the title of this book: Trump, he said, 'will make a comeback.'[20]

Hollywood in a New Guise

Trump had always sought the spotlight. His first significant venture into show business was the Broadway play *Paris Is Out!* in 1970. He was twenty-three, just out of Wharton when he approached producer David Black and offered to pay half the $140,000 cost of production. In return, Black would teach him the Broadway ropes—and Trump would receive equal billing in *Playbill.* The show ran sixteen previews and ninety-six regular performances before Trump and Black lost their shirts.

By the 1980s, Trump set his sights out west. He took an interest in buying the fabled Beverly Hills Hotel, even announcing he had hired Steve Rubell and Ian Schrager of Studio 54 fame to

---

18   Johnston, The Making of Donald Trump, p. 93.

19   Poniewozik, Audience of One, p. 62.

20   Barrett, Wayne. *Trump: The Deals and the Downfall.* New York: HarperCollins, 1992. p. xvi.

run it. But Trump's efforts to lowball the landmark failed miserably. "He was never a serious contender," said one of the owners. Next, Trump proposed building a world-record-setting 125-story skyscraper over the site of the famed Ambassador Hotel. He had joined a syndicate that bought the 23.5-acre lot for $64 million. But the Los Angeles Unified School District countered with a better deal. Later, Trump charged that the district had taken the land from him "as viciously as in Nazi Germany."

Trump then pitched a TV special—*Donald Trump Presents the Most Beautiful Women in the World*—to ABC head Roone Arledge. Trump boasted: "I'll bet it gets one of the top five highest ratings of the year!" The show did not make it past the pitch stage.

As Orson Welles learned in the twentieth century, buzz was all important. What Trump understood beyond all things is that, despite setbacks and rejections, you have to keep your name in lights. From his mentor, famed and later disgraced attorney and New York power broker Roy Cohn, he learned that even bad media is good media. There is no bad news—as long as they spell your name right! Indeed, Trump would become master of the media that has prevailed in the twenty-first century. The buzz, the hype, the glitz was what led him to *The Apprentice* and his new role as super-successful businessman. Kane, too, kept himself relevant with screaming headlines.

So, when Trump's contract as host of the enormously popular television show was not renewed in 2015, Trump made his boldest move of all. It was time to find a new character to play. He ran for president! And won! How did a Hollywood reject, a man known as both a compulsive liar and a friend to the forgotten man, win the top prize?

Some say Barack Obama is responsible for Trump's steely determination. Perhaps in some ways Obama exposed what Trump was not. Though they shared ambition, Obama was a real Ivy Leaguer, articulate, and comfortable with himself, which would all come through at one event. At the 2011 White House Correspondents' Dinner, Obama provided the inciting incident that convinced Trump, then flirting with politics, to run. At first, Trump reveled in the moment as he mingled with luminaries. Then the humiliation began as Obama proceeded to roast Trump mercilessly.

It was clear that Citizen Trump, the rehearsed TV boss, lacked the gift for witty and nimble repartee or acting the gracious guest, skills at which Obama excelled. The jokes stung because they pricked Trump's deepest insecurities. They cast him not only as a wannabe political player but as an inflated TV star. Obama lampooned Trump's gaudy taste in décor. He mocked his fixation on the false rumor that Obama was born in Kenya.

The powerful man as seen on TV was no longer in control. After dinner, Trump quickly left. He appeared bruised, apparently unable to take the criticism he regularly dished out to others. Instead of discouraging Trump, however, it triggered a taste for revenge. He needed to be taken seriously and regain stature among the Washington elite. To those who know him best, Trump's desire to run for president had been simmering for decades. But that public humiliation was just what he needed to light the fire. In 2015, Trump the showman would make the transition to politics complete.

07

08

CAM

— SNOW FALLING
OR TRANSITION

2. A MODERN-DAY KANE

You're right, I did lose a million dollars last year.
I expect to lose a million dollars this year.
—Kane

Charles Foster Kane seemed a natural hero for Trump—a boy born into affluence seeks attention and aspires to run for the highest office. The film weaves a story of a vain millionaire who collects statues, gardens, palaces, diamonds, and women. It exposes how Kane's life of empty acquisitions was a yearning for something much simpler lost in his childhood. After a life of fame-seeking, broken relationships, and self-isolation, Kane discovered firsthand the wisdom of Solomon: "All is vanity." He comes to realize that at the point of death, possessions and accolades could not save him. He wanted only one thing in the world: the humble sled he played with as a child! But why a sled?

Kane's treasured sled appears at the beginning of the story during one of the boy's happiest moments, the last item he held before being taken from his mother's comfort and love. It reappears as the story ends, burned in a heap with Kane's other possessions after his death. The final word, "Rosebud," underscores how alone he is. Even Kane's journalist team drifts off into speculation about the true meaning of his life. How could such a powerful man be so mired in a simple memory?

Someday, if a film was to be made on Trump, would the time spent on his train set in his Queens basement with his siblings perhaps provide a symbol for his own innocence as a boy in the suburbs before his move to the city to build an empire?[21] Might the trains have provided those memories in miniature, manageable in early life that later become the real railways that carry one across the Hudson river and into the life of power, identity, and adulthood?

As the story unfolds, there is the rise of the hopeful, almost carefree Kane willing to throw caution to the wind and make his media empire work. But gradually, there is a sense of malaise as we see a man isolated. He shuts out those voices, including his wife Emily's, that might (with a moment of self-awareness) shatter his glass menagerie made of purchased glamour. And as columnist David Brooks said of Trump, "His vast narcissism makes him a closed fortress."[22]

Citizen Kane, though structured in a grand riddle, for reasons of plot is not a mere detective story. Behind the crime scene

21   Kruse, Michael. "The Mystery of Mary Trump." *POLITICO*, November 6, 2017. Web.
22   Hufbauer, Benjamin. "How Trump's Favorite Movie Explains Him." *POLITICO Magazine,* June 6, 2016. Web.

are the echo chambers of Kane's lost childhood, with children's voices reverberating on the snowscape. It is an investigation into the missing person of his inner self, hidden behind the mask of the supposed powerful man. In the end, it is a portrait that is as much Welles as it is Hearst. How would it not be? Only something familiar could be so personal.

To that point, Trump's gut instincts can be traced back to the rough-and-tumble world of New York real estate and to loss—his father's influence, his mother's emotional absence, and his wounded life as an outsider. By most accounts, the senior Trump was ruthless, a tyrant, tough on his kids and singularly focused on whether they were "making bank." In other worlds, a man hardened by the desperations of the "old world."

Donald's older brother, Fred Jr., would take most of the heat growing up, and Donald resolved not to cross their father. Even so, Trump's outer-borough heritage and his father's callous admonition to be not only a king but a killer—something "big"—did not fully embolden Trump. Instead, it left him feeling trapped in a world that was too limited and narrow. Fred Trump warned his son not to go into Manhattan and not to go into debt. New York politician Andrew Stein wrote, "There's a big difference between Donald and Fred. . . . Donald was a showman from the get-go. He always loved the publicity and attention. [Fred] came to see me and said I should stop The Donald from getting so much publicity when he first started."[23] And despite the senior Trump's success with a thousand or so small rentals in Queens, Brooklyn, and Staten Island, the younger Trump concluded the effort came up short. By his assessment, Fred Trump, though a hard-ass, lacked the true killer instinct of Trump's later father figures, including Roy Cohn, political strategist Roger Stone, and Steve Bannon. What they all knew and in some way channeled was that Donald Trump was sui generis and would never fit into the establishment from which he was resoundingly rejected. Later, "Trump's strange orange hue, his combed-over thinning and dyed yellow hair, his 'yuge' tie and grating Queens accent made him especially foul tasting to the coastal elites."[24]

Trump's life became on some levels an embrace of his father's fire but a rejection of his father's goals, and that became the background he sought to escape. Fred Trump was the product of his own father's scandalous wealth. The nineteenth-century German immigrant, whose family name was Drumpf, struck it rich running a well-known brothel during the Gold Rush. The anglicized name itself presaged how Drumpf became success-

---

23   Salkin and Short, *Method to the Madness*, p. 40.
24   Hanson, *The Case for Trump*, p. 21.

ful. David Cay Johnston notes, "Bridge players definition of the word trump: a winning play by a card that outranks all others. But other definitions include 'a thing of small value, a trifle,' and 'to deceive or cheat' as well as 'to blow or sound a trumpet.' As a verb, trump means 'to devise in an unscrupulous way' and 'to forge, fabricate or invent,' as in 'trumped-up' charges."[25]

Eventually, he would be exiled from the U.S. on charges of corruption. His son Fred would marry Mary Anne MacLeod, whom Donald would later remember only in the most idyllic of terms. But with the revelations of his niece Mary Trump's first book, *Too Much and Never Enough*, it is apparent that she was not exactly as remembered by Donald. In reality, his mother, an immigrant herself, struggled with status and longed for the life of glamour, not at all uncommon to the American experience. Fred was "excited only by competence and efficiency," and Mary was captivated by "the dramatic and the grand." She had almost died during her youngest son's birth and afterward was regarded by many as unavailable and detached.[26] Unfortunately for Trump, that left the tenuous, no-frills connection with his father as the

---

25   Johnston, *The Making of Donald Trump*, p. 3.

26   Kruse, Michael. "The Mystery of Mary Trump." *POLITICO*, November 6, 2017. Web.

only nurturing semi-mentoring relationship and the one to manage the project called the making of Citizen Trump.

Like his father, Donald Trump built his reputation in real estate, but his real ambition was to build the Trump brand. The similarities with his dad are apparent. They were equally brutal in gaining ground. Donald built Trump Tower in 1983 by exploiting the "status of Polish workers to avoid payment, and it would wind up in a lawsuit." A federal court also found that "no payroll records were kept, no Social Security or other taxes were withheld and they were not paid in accordance with wage laws." In the end, Trump was so exposed that he was forced to settle for his shameless act in a contract dispute that partly defined his career.

While he exhibited familiar signs of the petty businessman looking for an advantage on immigrants or drywall or piping, Trump was more showman than behind-the-scenes entrepreneur. In truth, he was not building an empire of concrete but a story for cybermedia. "In the virtual landscape of TV and the movies, he was New York personified. He played the same character: a dashing, bemused man in a business suit or black tie, spending money, dispensing advice, insults, and baksheesh, creating a stir, turning heads, coming across less impressed with the characters he met than they were with him."[27]

It was hard for non–New Yorkers to understand that Trump, though he made a run at some promising projects, had a career that nearly ended before it began. Those in the know labeled him "Donald Trump, the demi-billionaire casino operator and adulterer" and mocked his pretensions for weighing in on world issues. Between the breakup of his marriage and the breakdown of his businesses, 1990 tends to be considered the low point in Trump's career. Some still believed that he was primarily a canny businessman, but it was in the 1990s when playing "Donald Trump" became his full-time job.[28]

Even then Trump was pegged as a destroyer more than a builder. The real key to his success was his ability to raise funds and put on a big show. Trump fits the archetype of so many casino-selling, lick-and-a-prayer millionaires, which is one of the pitfalls of a capitalist nation. He could turn a wounding failure into a commodity. When the numbers do not compute, the numbers need to be spun into a narrative of future promise with a perpetual rollover of interest. In *The Art of the Deal*, he says, "Being good in business is the most fascinating kind of art.

---

27   Poniewozik, *Audience of One*, p. 68.

28   Ibid, p. 63–64.

Making money is art and working is art and good business is the best art."[29]

Many who knew Trump would claim his art of the deal was more like the art of the steal. Trump was "astonished," Wayne Barrett, the crusading writer of the *Village Voice*, wrote, "that he suddenly seemed to have the same impact in a Citibank board-room that he'd once had on the Donahue show."[30] Phil Donahue was an early skeptic.

Trump's facade of living the dream was largely fiction. The underbelly of these years building his legacy was laced with borderline criminal activity and shifty dealings. When it came to his foray into Atlantic City casino ownership, "Unpaid bills were cause for the Casino Control Commission to cancel the casino ownership license, take control of the casino, and have it run by trustees until a buyer was approved.[31] Donald Trump was saved—saved by the government, deeming him, once again, Too Big to Fail.[32]

Yet, if you see Citizen Trump in light of the rise and fall of Citizen Kane, you realize that his worst failures were about to fuel his comeback! Film critic Neal Gabler writes in *Life: The*

29   Ibid, p. 54.

30   Ibid, p. 61.

31   Johnston, *The Making of Donald Trump*, p. 86.

32   Ibid, p. 93.

Movie that "the celebrity-comeback story follows the arc of Joseph Campbell's 'hero with a thousand faces.' An extraordinary person surmounts extraordinary forces and returns to share rewards with his fellow man. Just so, 'the celebrity loses it all, a victim of his own hubris or of the public's fickleness.'"[33] Robert McKee explains, "This dilemma confronts the protagonist who, when face-to-face with the most focused forces of antagonism of his life, must make a decision to take one action or another in a last effort to achieve his Object of Desire."[34]

"Only then, after he has been forced to win back his fame, does the celebrity reemerge from Hollywood, if only figuratively, in magazines and books and television talk shows, sadder but wiser, to tell the rest of us what he has learned."[35] Trump would later say, "Anyone who thinks my story is anywhere near over is sadly mistaken."

Orson Welles, in his treatment of Hearst, offers the pieces of a puzzle that was the life of Charles Foster Kane and works them into a completed picture that reveals the person behind the persona. Where Welles ends and Hearst begins, or where Kane ends and Trump begins, is the mystery of this tale and worth

---

33   Poniewozik, *Audience of One*, p. 81.

34   McKee, *Story*, p. 304.

35   Poniewozik, *Audience of One*, p. 81-82.

investigation. No longer do we have mere film moving through a projector or a news headline; we live in an exploding hyper-real media universe, and it is often difficult to separate the real from the unreal. Which is why the comparison to an archetype like Kane is the useful tool to parse our president.

Is Donald Trump a modern-day Charles Foster Kane? Like Kane, he has spent a lifetime chasing fame and fortune and relevance. Is the escalation of the role of wealth in modern society a blanket to cover childhood hurts? How could Trump, when worth even an exaggerated few million or even the billions he still claims, still feel like an outsider? Someone who does not belong? Kane in the film confesses, "I always gagged on the silver spoon."

The adult Trump, like Kane, is meticulous in the crafting of his public persona. In their rise to the top, it is easy to trace similar patterns. With a close study of Kane and his formula for exaggeration and hyperbole, Trump's arc is predictable. The techniques that had worked for audiences in Kane's time—railroad stops, newspapers, even fuzzy radio and TV—were replaced and amplified by Twitter, Facebook, and nonstop cable TV on giant screens. But the messages don't change.

Trump may have even had his Rosebud moment, though of the twenty-first century variety. Kane whispers the mysterious "Rosebud" and Trump tweets his nonsensical "covfefe." Like the reporters at Kane's deathbed, the entire world scrambles for answers to the meaning of Trump's cryptic message. Once there, the tweet became a communications cul-de-sac that commanded mass media attention. Kane created his own frenzy in his screaming, attention-grabbing newspaper headlines.

We are fixated on this spectacle, on the man's lashing out, misdirecting, or his need for affirmation. Trump intrigues us. The obsession with his every syllable also says something about the character of the media. Jean Baudrillard, in his book *Simulacra and Simulation*, says, "We live in a world where there is more and more information, and less and less meaning." Not so long ago, news programs had a standard of objectivity, but now with Trump, cable news (with the exception of Newsmax and to a lesser degree Fox) and much of print media had set him up to fail. Trump was being framed in advance.

There is an echo of Kane in the way Trump faces down the media—a.k.a. the Beltway, the Swamp, the Deep State. And that's just the start of it. Kane had no shame in saying he bought the media to change the nation's opinion. "Six years ago," he says in the film, "I looked at a picture of the world's greatest newspapermen. I felt like a kid in front of a candy store. Well, tonight, six years later, I got my candy—all of it. Welcome, gentlemen, to the *Inquirer!*"[36] We also see Kane manufacture a war in Cuba to sell more papers, with a shockingly made-up story. In newsreel footage, as is common to all world leaders, he shakes hands with Adolph Hitler, as we might see Trump shake hands with Kim Jong-un, Vladimir Putin, or Xi Jinping. Afterward, Kane tells America, "You can take my word for it, there will be no war." In short, we see Kane as a man for whom everything— from the rule of law to the truth of what's printed in his papers— can readily be bent, and without guilt, in the service of petty quests: for revenge, power, and, ultimately, a love of the people.

Trump's rise to fame prior to his appearance on the world stage was filled with improvisation in the persona he fashioned for tabloid coverage, even taking on WrestleMania, which was less sport than pure reality TV show.[37] "It asks you to invest your

---

36   Mankiewicz, Herman J., and Orson Welles. "Citizen Kane (1941)." *Best Film Speeches and Monologues*. Filmsite. Web.

37   The public largely saw a rambunctious sybarite who marketed glossy apartment buildings under the label of accessible luxury; flaunted his yacht, airline company, and professional football team; and partied with entertainers and models even though he was married. Appearances at WrestleMania, on *The Howard Stern Show* and *Late Night with David Letterman*, and in various films implanted him in the public consciousness in the 1990s.

very real emotions into real people, all while being aware of the inner workings of the machine that drives the entertainment. Any fan of the squared circle has heard the phrase, 'You know wrestling is fake, right?' and a modern reply is usually some version of, 'Yeah, so is *Game of Thrones*.'"[38] The same showmanship was apparent in the sensational nature of Trump's campaign rallies, where it is possible that the symbolic speech or acts for the collective can run wild and even out of control.

But before his rallies, when he first attempted his climb onto the national stage, his outward hubris would be matched by his humiliation at the hands of the national press corps and his fellow Republicans. The rejection would drive him deeper into the tough-guy shadow persona he had forged in the casinos, the boardrooms, and the mean streets of New York and Hollywood. Trump was still searching for his ultimate starring role. His rocky path to the top would be cleared by *The Apprentice*. As Trump said, "I enjoy my successes much more because I realize it wasn't so easy after all."[39]

---

38   Pagliei, Christa. "Reality TV and Wrestling - A Closer Connection Than You May Think." *Pro Wrestling Stories*, December 12, 2020. Web.

39   Poniewozik, *Audience of One*, p. 82.

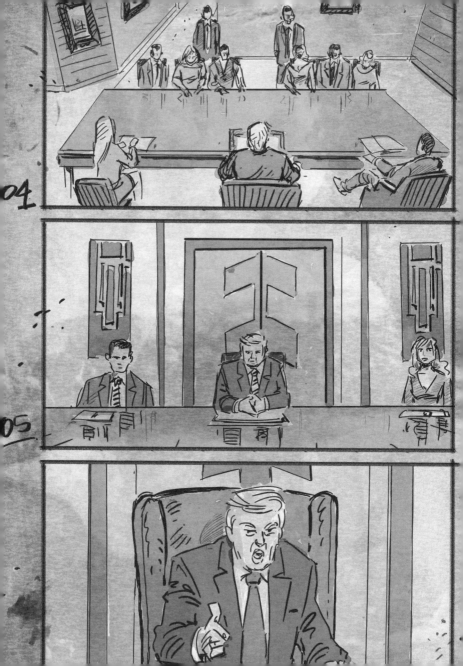

3. REALITY TV KINGPIN

Sure we're speaking, Jedediah . . . you're fired.
—Kane

That's what we see Kane tell his oldest and only friend, Jedediah Leland: "You're fired!" Sound familiar? Donald Trump during his *purgatorio*—his failure as businessman and real estate entrepreneur and being denied the big screen—has strutted across the small screen in a decades-long media performance to sustain his image. To view him without understanding how the media works and his strategy for doing "air time" battle is to miss the reasons behind his rules of engagement. He was nothing without the big (and small) screen; this was his stage to win a war. A war that had been raging for decades and was now about to reach a crescendo.

We may be astute about politics and power but often miss the evolution of media and how it continues to impact our perception. Trump was born in 1946 at the dawn of the American broadcast era while Hollywood was riding high. One can think of the big 1940s flashing neon movie marquees, black-and-white announcements of *Citizen Kane*, and the birth of the genius Welles. Today, however, media operates no longer in the fixed storytelling of a dark theater to an audience of hundreds but rather the unbridled, fragmented information that pops up on a billion cell phones. The line between reality and the simulation of reality has been blurred. Baudrillard observed, "Actual nature, seen in person, disappoints next to impeccably shot nature documentaries." And Donald Trump the simulacrum, the performance, had in Baudrillardian fashion eclipsed Donald Trump the businessman—so much so that the former would have to bail out the latter."[40]

To understand Trump is to approach him less through the lens of a psychologist or political thinker and more as a TV critic. Growing up, TV was Trump's touchstone. He was not alone. The public was eager to consume what the networks provided, even a national platform for religious programming. "Television became a kind of church itself in the 1950s, with televangelists like Fulton J. Sheen, the Catholic bishop and host of *Life is Worth Living*, and Rex Humbard, the guitar-strumming preacher. Trump later recalled watching Billy Graham's televised Crusades "for hours and hours" with his father.[41] Trump biographer Michael D'Antonio writes. "Fred was also, as Donald would eventually

---

40   Poniewozik, *Audience of One*, p. 64.
41   Ibid, p. 6.

be, a fan of the Reverend Norman Vincent Peale, a Christian pro-to-Oprah who ministered on radio and TV and whose *The Power of Positive Thinking* presented Christianity as a kind of self-help salesmanship guide."[42]

Kane underwent a similar transformation. In the film, he is cast as a well-intentioned do-gooder who seeks to ride his self-aggrandizing ambition to fame for the sake of the forgotten American. He began as a progressive (and was called a communist), but after failure at the ballot box, he became a reactionary and was accused of being drawn to fascism—language we hear from media and protestors against Trump today. As Leland said of Kane, "I don't suppose anybody ever had so many opinions. He never believed in anything except Charlie Kane. He never had a conviction except Charlie Kane in his life." Interest in objective truth was secondary, but like Trump he understood that most people might be persuaded by the art of the delivery. Whether he knew how to connect as does Trump, the fact is that "the trick of salesmanship, to use the polite term, is not to fool your audience. It's not to get them to fool themselves. Once they've bought in, they'll ignore an uncompleted border wall the way heavily invested tenants, wanting to believe they made a smart purchase,

---

42   Ibid, p.10.

will ignore the bad fit on a kitchen fixture. In a speech to the VFW, Trump told his audience to disregard any negative news about him: "Just remember, what you're seeing and what you're reading is not what's happening."[43]

The question for Americans is, regardless of party, at what point of the performance does the power of personality morph into an autocratic personality cult? When does it undermine our long-term precedents for the rule of law and the checks and balances put in place to prevent corruption? Those are the very things warned by Hannah Arendt in *The Origins of Totalitarianism*. Stephen Colbert expressed a version of Arendt's idea on *The Colbert Report* when he defined "truthiness," a term for the bastardized reality when feeling becomes more important than thinking. James Poniewozik puts it well: "We are divided between those who think with their head and those who know with their heart."[44]

A vivid version of those thoughts is manifested in Kane, who admittedly used his newspaper machine to control public opinion. In an art-imitates-life moment, news of the sinking of the battleship *Maine* was splashed across Kane's daily. "Fake news" did not begin with Trump's election to the presidency,

43   Ibid, p. 247.
44   Ibid, p. 247.

though. Nor did it originate with the modern twenty-four-hour news cycle and social media that encourages half-truths or outright falsehoods in order to stay up to the minute with the most recent current events. In fact, many historians trace the origins of fake news to the beginnings of the Spanish-American War. Historian and author William C. Kashatus writes, "At the turn of the 20th century, fake news was called 'yellow journalism,' or sensationalizing the news with inflammatory cartoons and exaggerated accounts in order to sell more newspapers. No newspaper did this better than Joseph Pulitzer's *New York World* and William Randolph Hearst's *New York Journal*."[45]

Of course, the fine print would reveal that the newspaper account of the sinking was due to a boiler explosion, not hostile fire, but the story stoked further hatred of Spain, and the war was on. Kane knew that scandal, as well as war, sells newspapers, so he printed an illustration of a young woman, her naked rear end showing, forced to strip before Spanish agents. The headline read: "Does Our Flag Shield Women?" The article concluded, "Reporters following up on the story later learned that the Spanish agents had used matrons to do the undressing, and, as

45   Kashatus, William C. "This Was a Real 'Fake News' Story – And It Landed Us in a War." *History News Network.* Columbian College of Arts & Sciences, February 26, 2018. Web.

proper gentlemen, they never viewed the woman's naked body themselves. No matter: She became a cause célèbre for the war hawks."[46] In real life, Hearst would write, "The public is even more fond of entertainment than it is of information," and he used fake news.[47]

Kane's bravado finds echoes in Trump's. Kane made headlines, many of them lurid, with his newspapers. Trump agitates via Twitter. Both Trump and Kane set off media earthquakes. The media waited with bated breath for Kane's every utterance, just as they do for Trump's next tweet. One major difference might be that Citizen Trump creates the conflict that causes the networks to engage in for ratings, whereas Kane merely bought all of his competition.

There is another curious link between Trump and Kane, and Welles himself. Here's how Welles later recalled that episode: "Roosevelt encouraged me to run for senator of Wisconsin, my home state, which is in the hands of very reactionary milk producers. But as a leftist, I had no chance at all. And I cowardly declined, especially because I was divorced. Well, who was elected but the dreadful Joseph McCarthy. Today I tell the story saying

---

46   Charles River Editors, *Hearst, Welles, and Citizen Kane*, p. 18.
47   Todd, Richard. "America's Original Fake News." *HuffPost, May 1, 2017. Web.*

that if I had run, McCarthyism would never have existed!" As McCarthy rose to power, alongside him as chief counsel was a young lawyer named Roy Cohn, who we know would figure prominently in Trump's life.

"I hear Roy in the things [Trump] says quite clearly," Cohn's partner told the *New York Times*. "If you say it aggressively and loudly enough, it's the truth—that's the way Roy used to operate to a degree, and Donald was certainly his apprentice."

"You knew when you were in Cohn's presence you were in the presence of pure evil," said lawyer Victor A. Kovner, who had known him for years. Cohn's power derived from his ability to scare potential adversaries with lawsuits. Trump has been a party in more than 3,500 lawsuits, some of them accusing him of civil fraud.[48] Trump would remain loyal to Cohn for many years. But as Trump would confide in 1980, even he was trying to distance himself from Cohn's inevitable taint. "All I can tell you is he's been vicious to others in his protection of me . . . He's a lousy lawyer, but he's a genius."

Cohn advised Trump to never settle, never surrender. Instead, counterattack, fire back twice as hard. No matter what happens, no matter how deeply into the muck you get, claim

---

48   Johnston, *The Making of Donald Trump,* p. 22.

victory and never admit defeat. New York columnist Liz Smith would conclude that Trump lost his moral compass when he made an alliance with Roy Cohn. A core lesson Trump learned from Cohn: to stay in power, every protagonist needs an enemy—real or imagined. Orson Welles hewed to that mantra in *Citizen Kane*, providing Jim Gettys as the archenemy of Kane. "Don't worry about me, Gettys. Don't worry about me. I'm Charles Foster Kane. I'm no cheap, crooked politician, trying to save himself from the consequences of his crimes."

Counter to that, some have observed Trump's kindness and openness to those biographers or staff writers who helped write his books. Or his fatherly touch to those who needed his help. One of his executive assistants, Norma Foerderer, tells of how Trump would open the mail and write $5,000 checks to strangers. Poppy Carlig, who was fired during season 10 of *The Apprentice*, thought "Trump had a TV personality and a non-TV personality. When the cameras are on, he's on, and he's very good at selling himself."[49] Those who know him would add that he converses with people on the lowest rung of the ladder, the cooks, the cleaners, who say he personally greets them by name regularly and asks specific details of their lives.

---

49   Salkin and Short, *Method to the Madness*, p. 107.

His critics would stipulate that his nice guy side was his only a disguise to cloak his ambition. He knew he needed to schmooze both the people and the powerful. Journalist Tony Schwartz, Trump's co-writer on the autobiography *Art of the Deal*, has described Trump as a man with little self-worth, who disguised his lack of personal confidence with financial status, yet still could not fill a "black hole." And so, in the boardroom, on camera, or on the campaign trail, he is unwilling to be ignored. As we see in Kane's portrait as Hearst, this trait becomes his final isolation and emptiness.

The Apprentice

Trump learned from Cohn that bad attention is good attention. If he was a failing real estate magnate in real life, he could play a wildly successful, scripted one on TV in *The Apprentice*. Even with scripts, reality TV required sharp instincts: the ability to sniff out potential conflict and to pit one opponent against another. This was a skill set that Trump practically invented. And, as a bonus, reality TV would help overlook his past of bankruptcies and reputation for stiffing workers. He could rebuild his persona. A *Newsweek* article captures this transformation with statements such as: "the most addictive new show on television," "a 15-episode infomercial for Trump himself," "not long ago,

Trump, 57, was a bloviating real-estate developer with a taste for young women and the spotlight. Today he's—exactly the same" but somehow "so cool." "His hair, his resurgence, and sometimes even his political views became part of the national conversation."[50]

Fourteen seasons as the bombastic host of *The Apprentice* provided not just a chance to increase visibility but to redeem his fame and his fortune, as many would learn later from his tax returns. But like Citizen Trump, even tax returns were nothing new in the case of the man behind Citizen Kane: Hearst. Joseph Thorndyke of Tax Analysts observes, "'Some of the most interesting commentaries on the more or less private lives of the famous stars of stage and the cinema are to be found in the income tax appeals which flow in a steady stream into the capacious mail box of your patient Uncle Sam,' a *Washington Post* columnist wrote in 1932. Indeed, the 1930s were something of a golden age for celebrity tax gossip, thanks largely to the New Deal and its focus on taxing the rich."[51] Beyond taxes or scandal, Trump, via a new television show, was becoming Citizen Trump. It also prepared him for his next role, that of candidate Trump. His real

50   Ibid, p. 160, 385.

51   Thorndike, Joseph J. "News Analysis: Tax Troubles of the Rich and Famous, 1930s Edition." Tax History Project. Tax Analysts, August 23, 2012. Web.

goal was a more lucrative contract with NBC. "To Trump, a man who reads the New York tabloids religiously," says David Cay Johnston, "I knew that just about the worst fate he could imagine for himself, short of death, would be waking up to these *Daily News* and *Post* covers: NBC to Trump: You're Fired."[52]

On the path to the election, he morphed into a social and political pundit on Fox News, famously offering opinions on everything from the Iraq War to Obama and birtherism. Like Hearst in newspapers, his objectives were not purely commercial because he also sought political power. Republican operative Sam Nunberg gave this early feedback on the man: "Trump does the birth certificate. I think it's politically genius. While it might seem that Trump's platform was born in 2015, the truth is that he had been voicing his political opinions for much of this life." And in parallel to Kane, he was not shy in sharing his opinions, which changed over time; he was not always the conservative he began to play.

Birtherism was also opening him up to accusations that he is a racist. David Letterman, in 2011, was the one of the first to take Trump seriously enough to call him a racist, in so many words, for pushing the smear that Obama was not born in the

---

52   Johnston, *The Making of Donald Trump*, p. xii (intro).

United States, even as serious news outlets indulged Trump as a harmless buffoon. "It's all fun. It's all a circus. It's all a rodeo," Letterman said. "Until it starts to smack of racism."[53] Kane's model Hearst would spread fears about the "yellow peril" of Asian immigration to stir up fear in his circulation.

The art of building a heroic persona comes with an initial reluctance to accept power, until wounded by the enemy and pulled into the arena. Trump was well aware of this, as is clear in an interview with Chris Mathews:

> Chris Matthews: Why don't you run for president?
>
> Donald Trump: People want me to all the time.
>
> Chris Matthews: What about you?
>
> Donald Trump: I don't like it. Can you imagine how controversial I'd be? You're thinking about [Clinton] with the women? How about me with the women?[54]

In truth, Trump had flirted with politics for decades, but mostly for book sales and free PR.[55] He did push his credentials a bit further with the Reform Party in 2000, seeking advice from then Minnesota governor Jesse Ventura, but he knew Pat Bu-

---

53   Poniewozik, *Audience of One*, p. 79.

54   Salkin and Short, *Method to the Madness*, p. 8.

55   Sullivan, Kate. "Howard Stern: Trump's Candidacy for President Was a 'Publicity Stunt'." *CNN*. Cable News Network, May 23, 2019. Web.

chanan was unbeatable in a debate. In 2012 he toyed with the idea of running against Mitt Romney but instead launched his book, *Time to Get Tough: Making America #1 Again*, which was reissued under the new title *Time to Get Tough: Make America Great Again!* to match his 2016 campaign slogan. In 2014, he threatened to run for governor of New York but bailed out knowing he could not defeat Andrew Cuomo.

Before launching his campaign for president in 2015, Trump would be accused of being a political chameleon. He changed parties seven times and repeatedly reversed his position on key issues. Bob Woodward writes of Trump's stance on abortion in his book *Fear*:

> "You have a record of giving to the abortion guys, the pro-choice candidates. You've made statements. You've got to be pro-life, against abortion."
>
> "I'm against abortion," Trump said. "I'm pro-life."
>
> "Well, you've got a track record."
>
> "That can be fixed," Trump said. "You just tell me how to fix that. I'm—what do you call it? I'm pro-life, I'm telling you. Pro-life."[56]

---

56   Woodward, Bob. *Fear: Trump in the White House*. New York: Simon & Schuster, 2018. p. 3.

Trump, like Kane, would also be accused of being a Fascist, though they both spent most of their early career as supporters of the Democratic Party, but would step away once it was radicalized. In the end both men had failed as entrepreneurs and businessmen, and would need politics to keep their profiles to redefine their brand.

4. THE TRICKSTER CANDIDATE

You know, Mr. Bernstein, if I hadn't been very rich, I might have been a really great man.
—Kane

In the years before the 2016 election, the Republican Party placated Trump. It accepted his money and support, all the while failing to grasp his fervent desire to become a major force in American politics. Along the way, the party gave Trump the kind of legitimacy he craved, another uncanny parallel to the *Citizen Kane* strategy. Writing for MassLive, Ray Kelly says, "Donald Trump has called *Citizen Kane* his favorite movie, but classic film lovers have to wonder if the GOP nominee hasn't lifted some of his campaign strategy from the Orson Welles masterpiece."[57] Clearly both Kane and Trump were the sons of inheritance, media business owners, and sought political relevance.

Repeatedly underestimated prior to his actual run in 2016, Trump muscled his way into the Republican elite by force of will. He had badgered Mitt Romney into accepting his endorsement on national television, and Trump became a celebrity fix-

---

57   Kelly, Ray. "'Citizen Trump' - Similarities between 2016 Campaign and Orson Welles Movie." *MassLive*, October 12, 2016. Web.

ture at conservative gatherings. He abandoned his normally tight support wallet and wrote five- and six-figure checks in a bid to garner clout. He courted conservative media as deftly as he had the tabloids. Trump quietly met with Republican pollsters who tested his message and gauged his image across the country.

Pollster Kellyanne Conway conducted a survey that showed Trump's negative ratings were sky-high. She advised him that there was still an opening for him to run. John McLaughlin, another pollster, drafted a memo that described how Trump could run as a counterpoint to Obama in 2012 and outshine Romney. Roger Stone wrote a column on his website envisioning a Trump candidacy rolling to the nomination, powered by wall-to-wall media attention.[58] But after all that preparation, Trump rejected two efforts to "draft" him. He was not prepared to abandon his lucrative television career. In mid-May 2011, Trump announced he would not run for office and canceled a speech at a major Republican fundraiser in Iowa.

Having stepped back from a campaign of his own, Trump would look for relevance through Mitt Romney's bid, but his determination to seize a role for himself collided with the skepticism of those he approached. While he saw himself as an im-

---

58   New York Times. "Donald Trump's 2016 Bid for President Began in an Effort to Gain Stature." *Tampa Bay Times*, March 13, 2016. Web.

portant spokesman on economic issues and a credible champion for the party, the Romney campaign viewed him as a mere attention-seeker with no political gravitas.

In September 2011, Romney half-heartedly made the trip to Trump's Fifth Avenue high-rise. The decision to court Trump was twofold: a desire for fundraising help and the conviction that to shun him would be more dangerous than building a relationship with him. The test of that strategy came in January 2012, before the make-or-break Florida primary. Trump wanted to endorse Romney at a local Trump property. Romney aides chose to avoid a spectacle.

"The self-professed genius was just stupid enough to buy our ruse," said Ryan Williams, a former spokesman for the Romney campaign. In his remarks, Trump insisted that the campaign had lobbied for his support strenuously and described his own endorsement as Romney's biggest of that year. The campaign denied both points. And Romney refused Trump's demand for a prominent speaking role at the Republican National Convention. When Romney lost the election, Citizen Trump was taking notes for another day.

As the 2016 election approached, Trump reached out to talk radio. Welles, in his preparation to play Kane, stated, "There is no place where ideas are as purely expressed as on the radio . . . it is a narrative rather than a dramatic form." [59] Trump would also connect with right-wing websites such as breitbart.com. He also befriended Reince Priebus, the Republican National Committee chairman, who was trying to rescue the party from debt. Trump gave hefty donations to super PACs supporting Republican leaders on Capitol Hill.

Lo and behold, on June 16, 2015, after a theatrical descent down the grand escalator at Trump Tower, Trump announced his candidacy. It was reflective of Kane's major announcement in the Grand Hall when he decided to put his opponent on notice that he would be running for office and that they should beware. In his remarks, after descending to the people, Trump punctuated the very themes he had laid out in a speech at the Conservative Political Action Conference five years earlier. "We are going to make our country great again," Trump declared, a slogan that was recycled from the Reagan campaign and that echoed the Kane (Hearst) America First. He, like Kane, was also speaking like a man of the people, saying, "I will be the greatest jobs president that God ever created." And so it began. He would recap-

---

59   Callow, *Orson Welles: The Road to Xanadu*, p. 373.

ture America's interest from Obama and decades of corporate interest in the Global Village.

Kane's (like Hearst) attempts to secure political office were also trickster-like, in that he was never committed to one party, but rather his own success. He served as member of the U.S. House of Representatives from 1903–1907. He ran for mayor and governor of New York, the U.S. Senate, and attempted to secure the Democratic nomination for president in 1904 but lost. As Trump used *The Apprentice*, Hearst used his publications to drum up support for his campaign, which included support for the Spanish-American War. Early on, Hearst (like Kane and Trump) was left-leaning, promising to be a champion for the working class, but later broke from the Democratic Party and became more conservative.

Trump's challengers underestimated his secret weapon: the ability to adapt and to connect with a crowd, a talent similar to Kane's that simply could not be overlooked. He repurposed his stagecraft as statecraft. Like Kane, Trump refashioned himself as the outsider willing to take on the establishment and clearly define the opposition. He railed against the left-leaning media, a perfect villain for long-term programming. This was a move by a shapeshifter who, like Kane, was in fact part of the media himself. Unlike other candidates who ran as outsiders, Trump was a known brand, and he knew how to keep his audience wanting more.

In his roles as outsider, change agent, and Trickster King (in Jung's lingo), Trump, like Kane, became the dirty fighter willing to join a brawl for a higher moral cause. In the process, he would strike blows against the presumed coronation of Hillary Clinton. He would challenge the country with a new formula that began with a well-fashioned persona and one that would blend politics with entertainment.

U.E.
St

TRU
+
MEL
ON
ESCA

LOW
AND

GO
ESCA

OVER
St

TIGH

5. TRUMP'S POLITICAL STAGE

I am not a gentleman.
I don't even know what a gentleman is.
—Jim Gettys (Kane's opponent)

Just as a theatrical player needs an enemy to battle, so too must the stage be set for a great rescue. Aside from his political foe, Gettys, Kane had the Great Depression, war, and the rising tide of communism to contend with. Trump had the all-too-real fear of terrorism, the continuing fallout from the 2008 recession, taxpayer bailouts, and a rising threat from China to American workers. If Jung were analyzing the moment, he might suggest that the politically correct were ignoring America's shadow: "Everyone carries a shadow, and the less it is embodied in the individual's conscious life, the blacker and denser it is," he wrote. "If it is repressed and isolated from consciousness, it never gets corrected."[60] The collective voice in this case had been underground.

The shadow loomed large in the wings of the 2016 Republican primaries. The comparison between Jeb Bush and Donald Trump was instructive. Compared to Trump, Bush came across

---

60   Myers, Scott. "Reflection on Carl Jung (Part 3): Make the Darkness Conscious." Go Into the Story. January 6, 2016. Web.

as tepid and meek on stage; he asked for mannerly apologies. Trump, on the other hand, refused to apologize. He bullied Bush, Cohn-style. Jeb was accustomed to polite society. Trump was a barbarian by contrast. Viewers across the spectrum watched as the anointed one was devastated by a shameless competitor, and in a style more game show than debate. Not even nasty and for-midable contenders, such as the studied Harvard debater Senator Ted Cruz or the highly touted Senator Marco Rubio, could shake Trump. His strategy was simple: *no rules*, down-and-dirty mud fight—insult, insult, and insult again. For now, reality TV would trump public policy.

As Kane did with his mastery of yellow journalism, Trump would tweet innuendo or even make things up and repeat claims when he could not win on content. And he engaged in charac-ter assassination: He claimed Cruz's Cuban-American father worked with Lee Harvey Oswald and asserted that Ben Carson was diagnosed with brain issues. Trump gave opponents snarky nicknames like Little Marco, Low-Energy Jeb, and Lyin' Ted, a trick Bannon claims he learned from Jung's archetypes. You could brand them and that would stick in the minds of the audi-ence. Simple character branding made for good TV.

Antiheroes are necessary evils, willing to make moral compromises to fight against even more violent forces. In our era of media vigilantes Trump was the political Dirty Harry, a wild west in politics. He was there to remind us—like it or not—that sometimes when you fight the power it gets bloody. It is why we relish seeing the ambitious Kane defy his father figures and take on any and all doubters, as Trump would eventually do.

Finally the forces of Left and Right were going to meet on a stage to fight for television dominance. The media would be the referee, the audience, and the judge. Thanks to Trump, we knew all their names: "CNN, Fake News," "Con Cast," "MSDNC", and the "'failing' New York Times."[61] The Clinton/Trump debates provided a charged venue to battle for the American soul. Trump was about to call out those anti-Americans. A familiar script not used since Pat Buchanan and Ross Perot in their campaigns in 1992, 1996, and 2000. James Poniewozik explains, "Perot was proto-reality TV, at a time when reality TV barely existed outside MTV's *The Real World*. He had an anti-slick performative populism, bolstered by his claim to simply be doing the bidding of average Americans."[62]

---

61   Kight, Stef W. "Trump's Nicknames for the Media Companies He Loves to Bash." *Axios*, July 1, 2017. Web.

62   Poniewozik, *Audience of One*, p. 73.

Trump rightfully captured a nostalgia for a simpler, more bucolic time when the average worker had a chance at the middle class, with a home and a future. As media avatar, he was expressing a basic truth felt by millions: Make America Great Again! Trump's successful campaign, like Kane's failed one, was about turning back the clock to when all communities, urban or rural, were respected as voters. Kane had his Gettys and Trump had Hillary Clinton.

In a baffling response, Clinton's campaign settled on a tone-deaf slogan: America Is Already Great. The Left had departed its role as party of the people many years before and was now partnering with Wall Street, tech companies, and major media. They had become the Establishment. Victor Davis Hanson points to Aleksandr Solzhenitsyn's 1978 Harvard commencement address, when he warned the Western world had lost its civic courage, saying, "Such a decline in courage is particularly noticeable among the ruling and intellectual elite, causing an impression of a loss of courage by the entire society."[63]

Hillary Clinton was the default character for the elite. And she and Obama made clear in two remarks they would probably like to forget because they gave Trump such potent ammu-

---

63   Hanson, *The Case for Trump*, p. 73.

nition: Clinton talking about some of Trump's supporters as "a basket of deplorables," and Obama characterizing them as people who "cling to guns or religion or antipathy to people who aren't like them."

Trump was gritty and unfiltered. He did not hold back on any topic: the violence in America's inner cities, the "hellhole" of Chicago, his infamous history of alleged sexual assaults, the belittling of his opponents, and his overriding combative nature. Clinton tried to cast him as the brute, but it didn't work. People had already met the shadow and embraced his ugly side. The war between Trump and Hillary was not only political, it was a primal battle for our hearts and souls. If Trump could be branded as the erratic, crass father, then Hillary could be labeled the cold, judgmental mother. She came off as angry and tired; as Trump claimed, she didn't have the "strength or stamina" to be president. She didn't have the presidential "look." Or that in the previous campaign she was "schlonged" by Obama.[64]

Rewind eighty years ago as Kane tells the crowd, "Here's one promise I'll make . . . My first official act as governor of this state will be to appoint a special district attorney to arrange for the indictment of Boss Jim W. Gettys." Flash forward, Trump tells

---

64   Tur, *Unbelievable*, p. 239.

Hillary, ala Kane, "If I win, I am going to instruct my attorney general to get a special prosecutor to look into your situation."

He also exposed Hillary's demons, including Whitewater and her use of the Clinton Foundation while secretary of state to make quid pro quo deals with would-be donors. A master of the find-the-villain strategy, Trump chained Hillary to Bill's skeletons. Trump's morals and treatment of women may be uncouth, but at least at that point he had never been accused of rape, thereby creating a moral equivalency.

Trump knew how to handcuff Hillary to Benghazi and to the ghosts of her husband's career. Hillary was hit hard from the all sides. She was forced to stare into the face of a brazen, rebellious kid who would not take no for an answer. The same kid who, like the youngster Kane, has his own bad memories of an early life, abandoned by his mother for a life of great wealth and fame to be one of the established. As Kane felt toward the memory of his sled, Trump might have felt the same toward his train set in his Queens basement.

Jung might conclude in the American psyche that if Trump played the emerging shadow child, the trickster hiding his true motives, then Hillary Clinton was the Great mother painted as the dark mystery and power unwilling to admit her mistakes.

She was never wrong. She inspired awe and reverence. But in her clash with the trickster, she may appear to be the one that devours, even one to eat her own children. We cannot speculate much beyond this without the psychiatrist chair, but from all we know on Kane and Trump (and their types), separation or even recognition and acceptance of the mother figure plays a great role in their attempts to find individuation and acceptance with a mass audience.

The unsolved mystery in their early personal lives would lead to a series of other female relationships and leave open secrets for the media to discover, especially during high profile campaigns.

04.

05.

 ALTERNATIVE SHOT
WITH H. CLINTON

6. X-POSED BY THE MEDIA

I'm going to send you to Sing Sing.
Sing Sing, Gettys. Sing Sing.
—Kane

Leading up to the 2016 general election, rival campaigns and many in the news media still did not regard Trump as a serious threat. They predicted he would quickly withdraw from the race and fade back into TV land as he had done before. Because of his undisciplined style, they underestimated the intense prepping Trump had done throughout that spring. He took a half-dozen trips to the early voting states of Iowa, New Hampshire, and South Carolina. What most forget is his media opponents were operating with struggling enterprises, which would also be revived by their constant attacks on the reality TV candidate. As Victor Davis Hanson puts it, "Media moguls had no idea that they were helping to birth what they would soon rue as their own Frankenstein's monster, with a life force that they could soon not control and that would nearly destroy its creators."[65]

By the late fall of 2015, Trump secured his position of dominance by pronouncing an America First campaign, as did Kane,

---

65   Hanson, *The Case for Trump*, p. 21

with a message about immigration controls and trade protectionism. Kane had done so to avert the Americans joining World War II. Their isolationist policies during a time of great global impulse would lead to their accusations as Fascists. Nevertheless, Citizen Trump had at last gained the status he had long been denied. He seemed slightly vengeful of his mocking at the White House dinner as he spoke of the significance of what he had achieved. "A lot of people have laughed at me over the years," he said in a speech. "Now, they're not laughing so much." As Trump ascended, the GOP wagered it could tolerate his temporary intrusion. But not everyone was onboard.

In early October, after the release of the infamous 2005 *Access Hollywood* tape, the criticism from his nemesis, President Barack Obama, became more pointed. He questioned the Republican nominee's character. The New York satirical magazine *Spy*, which had memorably dubbed Trump "the short-fingered vulgarian," pegged him as a bloviating fraud, a Potemkin businessman.

Obama again weighed in at a news conference in Chicago. "It tells you he's insecure enough that he pumps himself up by putting others down," he said, "not a character trait that I would advise in the Oval Office. It tells you that he doesn't care very much about the basic values we try and impart to our kids. It tells you that he'd be careless with civility and the respect that a real vibrant democracy requires."[66]

In the end, the election would not rest on Trump's peccadillos. No amount of ridicule could topple him. His only kryptonite was in the exaggerated claims he made about his early successes. His opponents organized a concerted effort to unmask Citizen Trump, which mirrored the political maneuvering around Citizen Kane when he made his runs for office.

Film buffs will remember that Kane—the married entrepreneur, man of the people—was found with his mistress in an apartment. His opponent Gettys threatened to reveal the scandal for all the world to see if Kane did not drop out of the race to defeat him as governor. In response, Kane showed no regret, nor did he acknowledge the genuine blow that news of the affair was to his wife. It was the seminal moment that began Kane's demise and fall from power.

Kane had done exactly as Jung had warned, he had become his persona and forgotten the genuine man (or boy) behind the mask. The parts of his life that he discarded were showing up in the very dark, shadowy figure of a man who would demand pow-

---

66   Keneally, Meghan. "President Obama's Long History of Insulting Donald Trump." ABC News, November 10, 2016. Web.

er and live and love on his own terms. "The only way to love," he would later say.

Citizen Trump recognized Kane's folly in becoming his persona at the expense of the man. He went as far as to call Welles, Kane's creator, "totally f*cked up. He was a total mess."[67] But would Trump recognize the same folly in his own story? After all, in his interview with Errol Morris when asked what he would say to Kane, Trump responded, "Get yourself a different woman." Kane himself would be doubted by his best and only friend, Leland, as he reached his end: "You don't care about anything except you. You just want to persuade people that you love 'em so much that they oughta love you back. Only you want love on your own terms. It's somethin' to be played your way, according to your rules."[68]

Kane and Trump both were, in modern parlance, "caught on tape." But the world had changed with endlessly intrusive media and so few secrets. Kane is witnessed entering the apartment of his new female friend. Other than a few shared moments, and some flirty language in the film, we are left to assume that theirs

---

67   Winfrey, Graham. "Donald Trump Says Orson Welles Was 'Totally F*Cked Up' & a 'Mess' - But He Still Loves 'Citizen Kane.'" *IndieWire*, June 10, 2016. Web.

68   Mankiewicz, Herman J., and Orson Welles. "Citizen Kane (1941)." *Best Film Speeches and Monologues.* Filmsite. Web.

is clearly an affair. When Trump is caught in his October surprise, we hear him speak of his ability to grab women by their genitalia because of his status.

So, what does that say about what we have come to accept? Being caught in one of their worst moments could define a character and brand him for life, as it did Kane. But here's the catch: Trump's brash language and his treatment of women was already accepted as part of his character. He was not here to preach a sermon. Kane was undone by the Gettys machine once the affair was exposed in print. He loses his wife, his prestige, and even his support of the forgotten people. Trump, after a bold look into the camera, stares down his moral judges, quickly apologizes, and deflects to Bill Clinton and his well-known sins, using the strategy of blaming a more heinous character.

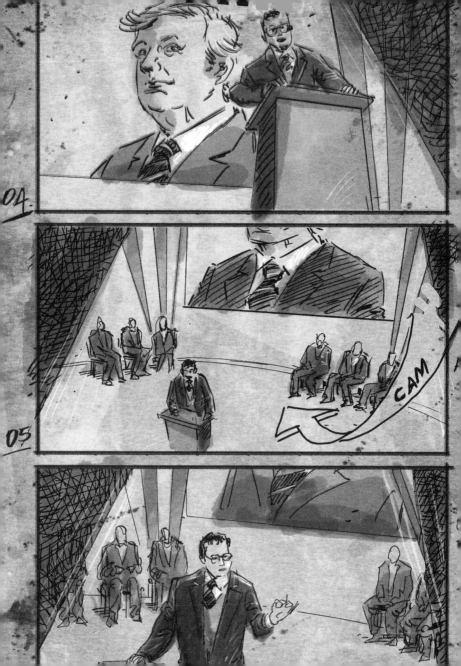

04.

05.

CAM

7. CHANNELING TRUMP

*There's only one person who's going to decide
what I'm going to do and that's me.*
—Kane

In the hyper-real media, Trump had the portfolio for the job, and political opponents found out the supposed blowhard was no joke. He was now aiming to bring show business to the executive office. He used the persona he had developed for *The Apprentice* and a Fox News series called *Monday Mornings with Trump*, which would garner upwards of three million viewers. His target for the presidency would be sixty-five million individual and embittered voters. The math was not just possible, it was probable. As the author Fran Lebowitz would later say, Trump was "a poor person's idea of a rich person."[69]

Trump needed to confront in the center ring not just "crooked" Hillary, the continued popularity of Obama, and the mainstream media but also academia, Hollywood, and Wall Street. To face this multifront opposition, Trump assembled his own media-savvy A-team: Roger Stone, Steve Bannon, and Roger Ailes, founder and former chairman of Fox News. Bannon stormed

---

69   Poniewozik, *Audience of One*, p. 119.

the early meetings and assured Trump that he had "metaphysical certitude you will win here if you stick to this script and compare and contrast" with Hillary Clinton. "Their message is Donald Trump is bad, and we're not Donald Trump. The rest of the message was race, gender, LGBT."[70] Then there was Trump's de facto campaign manager, son-in-law Jared Kushner, who happened to own the *New York Observer*.

Trump seemed headed to all but certain defeat in 2016. It's reasonable to conclude that again he would have taken a page from *Citizen Kane*—on the day after the election, he would have claimed some version of "Fraud at polls!" and sound the opening bell for his very own media empire. Either that or he would have followed in Charles Foster Kane's final footsteps— retreating, alone and humiliated, to his private Xanadu in Mar-a-Largo, which (given his loss in 2020) would seem to be his likely destination.

It hadn't when the Access Hollywood tape was released just before the election, and not even when the revelation prompted more women to emerge and complain about similar events and harassment. There was a woman on a plane, a beauty contestant, and a reporter for *People* magazine. The list would go on and

---

70   Woodward, *Fear*, p. 24.

on. When asked about affairs during the divorce from his first wife, Ivana, he pleaded the fifth ninety-seven times. His affairs and his cavalier attitude toward women were already fodder for late-night comedy. In a 1992 appearance, summing up how he'd sold off his assets as he faced potential ruin, Trump told David Letterman, "I sold the Trump Shuttle. I unloaded my wife." The audience howled.[71] By 2016, he still had not outgrown and overcome the old Donald, the pig. The same medium that had developed and secured Trump's persona could have destroyed it.

As for Trump's favorite film, in the opening of *Kane*, during the *News on the March* segment, we learn the record of the great Charles Foster Kane after his death: "Twice married, twice divorced. First to a president's niece, Emily Norton, who left him in 1916, died 1918 in a motor accident with their son. Sixteen years after his first marriage, two weeks after his first divorce, Kane married Susan Alexander, singer at the Town Hall in Trenton, New Jersey. For wife two, one-time opera singing Susan Alexander, Kane built Chicago's Municipal Opera House. Cost: $3 million dollars. Conceived for Susan Alexander Kane, half-finished before she divorced him, the still-unfinished Xana-

---

71   Poniewozik, Audience of One, p. 80

du. Cost? No man can say . . ."[72] Popularity, scandal, and mystery were always what they are today: news.

At the start of the TV era, another personal political scandal had played out in public: Richard Nixon's 1952 financial scandal. Nixon's disgrace was short-lived following a televised apology on the evening news, during which he famously cited his family's dog, Checkers. By contrast, and as dramatic proof of changing times, Trump delivered his confessional speech via Facebook, Twitter, and cable news, not from a modest studio setting but from the splendor of Trump Tower in front of a night-lit backdrop of skyscrapers. He has never felt the need to apologize for anything. Kane was unapologetic when his affair was made public. Trump, too, said he did not seek divine forgiveness because he has done nothing wrong his entire life, an oft-made observation so at odds with most basic teachings of the Judeo-Christian faith. It is one of the reasons why I am at a loss to understand any religious leader embracing him.[73] James Poniewozik reminds us that Trump Reality TV was a work in progress for generations, and like the extremely flawed Bill Clinton,

---

72   Mankiewicz, Herman J., and Orson Welles. "Citizen Kane (1941)." *Best Film Speeches and Monologues*. Filmsite. Web.

73   Johnston, *The Making of Donald Trump*, p. 209.

he too would need to overcome scandals (and his two impeachments) to keep an American base.

Decades of developing a hardened persona, mastering the media, and building a political machine unleashed the dark powers of the reckless male. It was all-out war. If politics were a den of wolves, Trump showed up as a lion. And as Niccolò Machiavelli aptly said about lions in *The Prince*: "The lion cannot protect himself from traps, and the fox cannot defend himself from wolves. One must therefore be a fox to recognize traps, and a lion to frighten wolves."

Trump advertised his darkest impulses before his audience. So why did he succeed? Perhaps the more important question is, how, for the first time in American history, did a person who lacked the moral stature and usual credentials of political or military experience become president?

The focus of any study on Trump as Kane should not rely solely on the subjects (men) themselves but on the context and values in which they existed. From Kane (Hearst), a culture that has extolled rugged individualism, and the ability to achieve such vast luxury and fame, in contrast to the one Trump found with a creeping socialism, and obsessive media joining forces with the state. In Kane success was the result of effort and in

Trump's era it was the result of cheating. George Bernard Shaw famously wrote that Hearst's San Simeon home (Kane's Xanadu) was "the place God would have built, if he had the money." The same might be said of Mar-a-Lago. Hearst, like Trump, aspired to be an actor. He had an appetite for luxury that matched his ambitions in business and politics. Hearst married two show girls. In real life, Kane's Susan Alexander was Hearst's Marion Davies. She was eighteen and Hearst was fifty-two. "[Trump and Hearst] were both described as unfit for high political office...they inspired vehemence among their critics, and in some respects, they both flouted convention and social norms," Dr. W. Joseph Campbell, a professor at American University, tells WNYC's "All Things Considered" host Jami Floyd.[74]

Kane and Trump were sui generis their own brands, news channels, in a world of transforming media. To understand them is to understand they do not fit neatly into conventional life categories. Their enigmatic personalities are what lures their audience. What they fail to reveal or admit is part of their appeal. They fashioned the ability to have affairs, but viciously defend or skirt around them to the public. In the end, all of their weakness-

---

74   WNYC News. "Donald Trump, Through the Lens of His Favorite Movie: Citizen Kane." *WNYC*, July 22, 2016. Web.

es, or potentially corrupt enterprises, pale in light of the fact that they have a grand mission and have been chosen by the people.

Four years later, we wonder: When might Citizen Trump have his final reversal of fortune? The avid audience awaits the high drama. Thus far, even censored by the media, and threatened by legal suits and business defections, Citizen Trump, unlike Citizen Kane, has prevailed with his faithful followers, and we don't know what he will do with his life and career after the White House. Will his flawed character ever take him down? Even the accusation of having started an insurrection?

8. THE FORGOTTEN AUDIENCE

*It's also my pleasure to see to it that decent, hardwork-
ing people in this community aren't robbed blind by a
pack of money-mad pirates, just because they haven't
had anybody to look after their interests . . .*
—Kane

Maybe none of us has the answer to the riddle that is Trump's story, but we must try to find it to understand ourselves. No longer are we a country in the light of Ronald Reagan's Shining City On a Hill, one that holds to an aspirational arc that bends toward the just or good. Obama's presidency unwittingly, and in the name of unity, would nearly shatter this legacy, and racialize middle American values. "The idea of protecting traditions and the continuity of a landowning and small-business middle class has been essential to classical Republicanism from Roman agrarians who built the Republic and defeated Hannibal to England's working-class citizens who resisted the siren songs of European revolutions from the late eighteenth to early twentieth centuries. In such a conservative tradition, the hallowed and vibrant middle class was more grounded than the often self-indulgent rich and more careful and commonsensical than the poor."[75]

75   Ibid, p. 161.

America First or Make America Great was not a slogan for paranoid nationalists but the very warning in George Washington's farewell address to avoid war and foreign entanglements. Something Kane and Trump not only preached, but truly believed. In this Pax America national borders mattered and provided both a needed boundary for peace, which proved essential in a shrinking globalized world. One that formerly provided two World Wars, the Cold War, and 9/11.

What was not recognized by the elites was that by the time Trump descended his escalator, the character, so like Kane's, had been fashioned. He was the powerful antihero descending from the heavens to give up his privileged life to become a man of the people. The producers of *The Apprentice* had orchestrated the spectacle. A cast of extras was hired to cheer at the event. Now the show.

Trump delivered his preamble to confront Obama's legacy wrapped around Hillary Clinton as a royal mantle for her coronation. Who will protect America from foreign-born Muslims? Though it was a restriction of travel from terrorist hot spots around the globe, Americans still held traumatic memories of 9/11, which had unfolded on live TV and fostered a desire for boundaries. American international goodwill had crumbled with the fall of the Twin Towers, and though Obama would be given the benefit of the doubt, after eight years, mistrust lingered in the Democratic Party.

The same sentiment of mistrust is echoed in Kane's speech to the working class when he declares that he has "one purpose only: to point out and make public the dishonesty, the downright villainy, of Boss Jim W. Gettys' political machine—now in complete control of the government of this state! I made no campaign promises, because until a few weeks ago I had no hope of being elected. Now, however, I have something more than a hope. And Jim Gettys—Jim Gettys has something less than a chance. Every straw vote, every independent poll shows that I'll be elected. Now I can afford to make some promises! The working man—the working man and the slum child know they can expect my best efforts in their interests. The decent, ordinary citizens know that I'll do everything in my power to protect the underprivileged, the underpaid, and the underfed! Well, I'd make my promises now if I weren't too busy arranging to keep them. Here's one promise I'll make, and boss Jim Gettys knows I'll keep it: my first official act as governor of this state will be to appoint a special district attorney to arrange for the indictment, prosecution, and conviction of Boss Jim W. Gettys!"[76]

Like his favorite film character, Trump spoke to voters who were living in what was considered condescendingly as "flyover country" with its loss of jobs to China and a raging opioid crisis that Trump claimed he could fix. Given the two choices and the history of Clinton corruption, enough people in key states apparently felt: let's just vote for that son of a bitch and Drain the Swamp! Although Hillary won the popular vote, Trump won the electoral votes in states where the people felt most derided.

Trump does have an easier time saying "I" than "we," as in "I alone can fix it." In a happier—though no less challenging—era, Ronald Reagan's slogan included the communal word "let's," as in "Let's Make America Great Again." Reagan's version implied that greatness comes not from individual defiance of the world—as in "Me," "the Man," "the Person"—but in the collective dream. E pluribus unum. Trump's universe is one of disunity: a controlled chaos that makes for good drama, but could also destabilize the American political system.

Trump's real life not only was modeled on *Citizen Kane* but in political ambition had surpassed the fictional character.

---

76   "Citizen Kane (1941)." *American Rhetoric: Movie Speeches*, 2001. Web.

Like Kane himself, who declared the whole world as his enemy, Trump would need to feed his base to survive; however,
once in office, he would have to stabilize a country fraught with
partisanship and expand beyond his base, which would mean
a whole new act.

He would need to play a less familiar role as healer, uniter,
and (in the face of a common enemy) a leader to the world. A
grand crisis would give him this chance to redeem his reputation
and shed his persona as trickster to play the goodly king. How
would he respond?

04.

05.

ALTERNATIVE SHOT
ORLANDO IN THE BALCONY

9. THE FACELESS ENEMY

People will think what I tell them to think.
—Kane

Trump slayed numerous dragons during his four years of his administration—some external and many of his own design. Between accusations of Russian collusion and the Mueller investigation, the Deep State posse of higher guns sent to eliminate the unfit mental patient,[77] as well as two impeachments, and a revolving door of staff and cabinet, Trump had more enemies than ever.

As Kane did to Leland, Trump fired his supposed friend and Goldman Sachs powerhouse Gary Cohn. As long as he had the bully pulpit, he could say to his national audience, "You're fired!" At every turn, Trump emerged victorious, and as he kept finding enemies real and imagined, the nation was left bleary-eyed and exhausted. His presidency was defined by conflict, grandiose claims, and the promise of a bright future, as was his life. He was still caught in his exaggerated promises, covered by

77   Vallejo, Justin. "Lincoln Project co-founder George Conway says Donald Trump shows nine symptoms of mental illness in new video." *Independent*, September 13, 2020. Web.

a contagion of media. The lack of distinction between personal lives, entertainment, and political office was the same tragic lesson of *Citizen Kane*.

Faceless Enemy

Citizen Kane is based on the life of William Randolph Hearst, publisher and politician of the first half of the twentieth century. But there's at least one detail that Welles made up: the story of Kane's mother. In the film, Kane's mother, played by Agnes Moorehead, abandons her young son to the care of a banker, Mr. Thatcher, to protect him from his abusive father—a story line that turns out to be closer to Orson Welles's life than Hearst's. In real life, Hearst's mother was quite attentive to her son. She traveled with him around the world to visit the great works of art and architecture. What is little known about Hearst's mother was that she also died from the Spanish Flu in 1919, in San Luis Obispo, CA. The young Hearst was the only one by her bedside.

Her death and the flu would have an impact on Hearst. At the time, ordinances would be put in place for mask wearing. On November 5, the *Tribune* reported: "Numerous arrests of mask offenders were made yesterday, in most instances the offenders being left off with a reprimand on promising to obey the ordinance in the future." Where the outbreak of this sickness first occurred is difficult to determine as it could have begun anywhere; however, by the time the raging disease had run its course, records show that no country had been spared. Prior to this pandemic, the distribution of news was slow, with the major newspapers concentrating on a war being fought in Europe, the Russian Revolution, and the arrival of the Americans in France.

While the sickness earned a small article in a few newspapers in early September of 1918, a week later the *Times* told of more than thirty thousand cases of the flu in Army camps throughout the United States. Hospitals throughout the country were filling with sick people, with most of them dying just a day or two after admission. Flu symptoms were listed in the newspaper. Doctors, making a determination that the flu was spread by contact, published notices of "How to Avoid the Disease."

After 2020, modern readers would not find this news unfamiliar. A new and formidably real enemy appeared that would also expose Trump's battle-tested tactics: a new virus. The coronavirus pandemic exploded in the early months of the year. By spring, it had all but undone Trump's political apparatus. In confronting COVID-19, the showman Trump tried all the familiar strategies: dismiss the truth, blame the media, and exaggerate his control over the disease. With only some exaggeration, he found a true enemy in China.

China was the source of the virus and did not report it to the rest of the world. Though he could point to the role China had played and covered up, Trump could not control the death tolls or his scientists. The performer in Trump unwittingly turned the daily task force briefings on the deadly issue into self-promotion words of hope for "tremendous" progress; however, in an interview with Bob Woodward, on tape, he confessed that he was aware of the virus's severity and his own lack of control. Most seriously, he offered false hopes in the face of catastrophe. He compared himself to Winston Churchill by stating that the prime minister had also offered hope during the dark days of World War II. That was true, but only after Churchill had leveled with the public about the dire threats the country faced. If ever there was a time to end the show and transcend party politics, this was the moment—if only Trump could resist the spotlight.

During a pandemic, it is high risk to have an entertainer and what appeared to be a lack of curiosity as caretaker, especially during an election year. Trump could not turn off the character, or transform his speech to meet the collective need. Character was destiny. Even Welles, a master actor himself, admitted that an actor "can eliminate from his own personality certain things which are wrong for a particular role, but he cannot add."[78] Trump's normally acceptable levels of showmanship played as self-interest, if not self-absorption, and a ploy for political survival at the expense of the people.

Like Kane's market crash, Trump would have his own, as a result of the pandemic, though the stocks would come raging back by the time he left office. In part by stabilizing the market by exploding the debt. The United States was on a trajectory to suffer debt, sickness, and death of historic proportion.[79] Trump was at a severe disadvantage. The virus did not have a face. He could not give it a nickname or attack its moral character. He would eventually call it the China virus, which was accurate, but death was the real enemy now.

Each night, the play would begin. The White House delivered its briefing to a captive audience (with a brief intermission after Trump mused about injecting bleach as a cure) of Americans quarantined from harm and all sense of normalcy. Would Trump transcend his fictional model in Kane? Truly show himself as a leader for generations to come? Could he call upon his persona

78   Callow, *Orson Welles: The Road to Xanadu*, p. 317.
79   As of the writing of this book, in the US there have been over 24,646,327 cases and 408,912 deaths.

as businessman, the TV executive, even his tough antihero to redeem his reputation as the Great American President? Trump continued to play his familiar role, tweeted his enemies and the press from the Oval Office, as people—lots of them—were dying. Trump's campaign instincts were no longer useful. He had won the job; now he needed to win over the people in a crisis.

As the virus spread, Trump's presidency was questioned. Though Trump did order partial shutdowns of air travel from China and Europe, his failure to respond with a federal mobilization to unify governors and provide needed virus protection and ventilators threatened, even his staunch supporters. He was warned that if the economy was not put on hold to prevent the spread of the virus, in key cities, it would infect the whole nation for months if not years to come. Tax cuts and hopeful hyperbole, even a market rebound, could not stop COVID-19 from stealing America's breath. His daily show was masking his true efforts and the genuine success with Operation Warp Speed: an effort between government and business to speed develop vaccinations, his best use of business instincts during the crisis.

Trump had a trust problem that did not suit the situation. All his strengths as a showman were exposed as weakness. His reliance on double messages and repetitive speech were downright dangerous. His history of bending institutions to his agenda or "alternate reality," would even be called out by his faithful Evangelical wing.[80] Antics that might delay peaceful transition of power and further expose the country to the ravages of the pandemic. He had started as a change agent. He was, as former secretary of state Henry Kissinger suggested in 2018, "one of those figures in history who appears from time to time to mark the end of an era and to force it to give up its old pretense,"[81] but this moment required the age-old human touch.

This wasn't like the war Kane faced. His fall from power was a result of market and military forces beyond his control. Trump could have stopped it sooner had he mobilized a national initiative to work with the states and combat COVID. Once the chaos of a pandemic started showing up in the media, Trump had only one strategy left: find enemies. In this case, he had The Communist Party of China. Trump had already earned his record of standing against China on abuses on trade and had a believable target. But no blame would stop the virus from becoming a national security risk. America no longer needed a reality TV

---

80   Stracqualursi, Veronica and Jason Hoffman. "Televangelist Pat Robertson says Trump lives in an 'alternate reality' and should move on from election loss." CNN, December 22, 2020.

81   Hanson, *The Case for Trump*, p. 2.

star. In the terminology of Jung, they now needed the archetype of a moral king. This was no longer television.

In 1964, Canadian philosopher Marshall McLuhan memorably said the medium is the message. He also stated, "Politics will eventually be replaced by imagery. The politician will be only too happy to abdicate in favor of his image, because the image will be much more powerful than he could ever be." In Trump's case, I would suggest the man is the medium. And his message turned out to be wrong for these trying times.

And in this final comparison, perhaps we can see the parting of ways between the Kane figure and that of Trump, though the final post-election script has not been written. In light of Trump's defeat in the 2020 election, in what might have otherwise been a landslide victory without the virus, worldwide riots, and the loss of millions of jobs, we now have our stepping off point. The lesson of Kane and Trump is that during a time of personal crisis, it is no longer about power, but people; not about self-interest, or party, but the common trust. Trump was a symptom not a cause of a much more insidious disease even worse than the virus or the media: a nation that loses its moral pact between power and the people. Trump, even after a lifetime in rehearsal, misread the room. Where the people wanted caution, Trump showed boldness; when they wanted empathy, he gave hope; and when they needed the real thing, he gave them reality TV. Does this moment in time point us to the Rosebud?

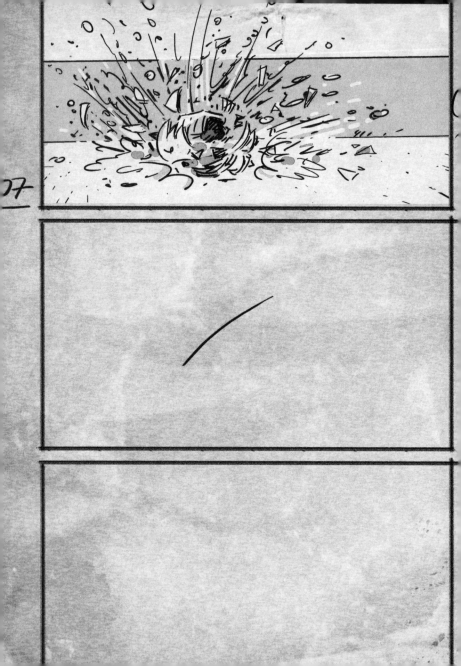

10. THE EMPTY BOX

*I don't think there's one word that can
describe a man's life.
—Jerry Thompson, investigative reporter
in **Citizen Kane***

Covfefe, unlike Rosebud, was not a scandal or a mistress. Perhaps Trump's real mistress is the media, a sordid affair that may ultimately force the American people to grapple with their reality, not the characters so much as their smartphones. So, do we follow Welles in Kane, as so many biographers to identify the culprit of tragedy as a lost childhood? We can imagine one of Trump's toy trains named Rosebud, perhaps being thrown into a furnace, symbolizing his lost years in New York City—years spent in aimless acquisitions with a desperate need to be noticed. Whether we can match the dramatic "Rosebud" device between Trump and Kane, we know it is only the symbol. Symbol of a loss of meaning or purpose, perhaps the American Rosebud.

Something fuels Trump's drive to need a spotlight that is never turned off. When his two ex-wives, Ivana Trump and Marla Maples, were asked by biographer Michael D'Antonio what makes Donald Trump tick, neither could answer the question.

When pressed further, Ivana said the only word she could come up with: "attention. He needs a lot of attention."

Trump appreciated what he understood to be the core insight of *Citizen Kane*: that wealth tends to isolate those who have it and that money doesn't always lead to happiness. Innocuous enough, you may be tempted to say, though profound by the standards we apply to Trump. Watch the film again and you'll realize Trump's analysis takes on a more frightening quality because he seems to think that *Citizen Kane* is about a great man who happened to fail, whose romantic relationships were less than ideal, and whose political career never panned out. What he overlooks is that the film is a tragedy, that shows pity for Kane's lost self. The film is about the rise *and* fall of a great man who denies his basic nature. Power and fame can follow achievement but cannot replace genuine love. Trump somehow misses the central narrative, which is a Faustian pact: a man, in pursuit of money, fame, and power, who ends up losing his soul.

The lessons become clearer every minute as the calendar page flips from 2020 to 2021, in light of the film. Having just inherited a fortune, the twenty-five-year-old Charles Foster Kane sets his sights on the newspaper business. He understands that by controlling the press, he can shape opinions on a mass scale—bending the truth as he sees fit. Over time, and through marketing savvy, he develops a powerful media empire. Because that's not enough, he then turns his sights to politics, running for New York governor as a stepping-stone to the White House. At campaign rallies, Kane gleefully brags about his poll numbers and vows to lock up his opponent, whom he condemns as the Establishment. Kane never gets to fulfill that pledge. Instead, he loses the election. His editors know what to do, and the following day their headlines scream, "Fraud at polls!" Sound familiar? But when does the gamesmanship with the media's complicity become a genuine threat to democracy?

Adrift from politics, the bored Kane turns his energies to the singing career of his second wife, a showgirl, whom he forces down a path of manufactured stardom. In the end, realizing she is merely the product of Kane's wishes and not her true self, she attempts suicide. Poniewozik reminds us of the stardom-seeking that drives Trump. On page seventy-five of *Audience of One* he writes, "Well, what the hell does Donald Trump do in this world? He has managed, through his face-saving deal with creditors, to hang on to the props of success and wealth. But being Donald Trump was never entirely about the money. It was about leaving his stamp—his golden T—on his age."

In his final reflections with interviewer Errol Morris, Trump either fails to see the moral emptiness at Kane's core or he does, and it doesn't strike him as exceptional.[82] Is Trump admitting that he's every bit as hollow as Charlie Kane? The same "empty box?" Every bit the narcissist and without the self-awareness of others? Is there someone in his inner circle who can penetrate the persona, or does he merely dismiss "those who do not see him as he sees himself?"[83]

Trump's worldview has always been rather dark. "Man is the most vicious of all animals," he has said, "and life is a series of battles ending in victory or defeat." Was his presidency just an Art of the Deal? Orson Welles described his character Kane as "corrupt," "damned," and "repellent," a man who "abuses the power of the popular press and challenges the authority of the law, contrary to all the liberal traditions of civilizations." A man who "has very little respect for what I consider to be civilization, and tries to become the king of his universe." Recall what his only friend Leland says about him after his death: "He never believed in anything except Charlie Kane."

---

82 Sharf, Zack. "Donald Trump Misinterprets The Themes of 'Citizen Kane' in Painfully Awkward Interview." IndieWire, November 17, 2016. Web.

83 Johnston, *The Making of Donald Trump*, p. 207.

Citizen Trump hasn't yet proved he is destined for a tragic fall as dramatic as Kane's, but surely the headline-hungry media will follow him until the end. The media virus feeds on fear and anger and human conflict, as it eats away at our civility in the name of entertainment and power. Hitler watched *Citizen Kane* and said it exposed everything wrong about America. People can be distorted by demagogues through media. Trump was in the white noise fighting a war with the only army he had: himself.

In the end, who's to say this writer isn't as subjective as Welles and merely putting on another show just to entertain you? After all, just like Welles did with Kane, I am finding something familiar in Trump. As an author and filmmaker, I spend many hours competing for airtime and needing the stage as a place where we remind ourselves we are not alone. George Welles, who was cared for by his young son Orson before his death from alcoholism, said, "We're born alone, we live alone, we die alone. Only through our love and friendship can we create the illusion for the moment that we're not alone."[84] Maybe that's why we read books and watch movies, even our holy ones, away from the noise of modern society, to know we're not alone.

---

84   Charles River Editors, *Hearst, Welles, and Citizen Kane*, p. 47.

Author Robert McKee states that "the dramatist is fascinated by the inner life, the passions, and sins, and madness and dreams of the human heart."[85] Maybe that is why I was always attracted to a dark theater, which enabled me to take a personal journey, not be merely a consumer in a commercial enterprise, or political partisan. Maybe it's the smell of popcorn, the sight of a latecomer caught in the rain. And then the lights go down, and you have a moment to remove your mask, breathe freely, and to enter into that persistence of vision, the exploration of human experience…

Fade in…

---

85   McKee, *Story*, p. 360.

MOTH
SIGN
THE P

FATH
CLOS
THE
WIN

APPENDIX

Trump on Jung
*[excerpt from book **How to Get Rich***
by Donald Trump, p. 78]

Read Carl Jung

I find reading psychology and self-help books useful. Carl Jung's theories fascinate me and keep my mind open to my own—and the collective—unconscious. Reading his books can also be a good form of self-defense. There's a lot we don't know about ourselves. Likewise, there's a lot we may not know about everyone else. Jung used the word psyche to refer to both the conscious and the unconscious processes. (That's where the word psycho comes from, by the way.) I first became aware of Jung through an acquaintance who had endured some extreme ordeals, yet he remained calm. I couldn't fathom where he got this sort of grace under fire demeanor, so I asked him, and he told me that Jung's ideas kept him centered.

My friend put it like this: Donald, I've learned from my experiences. As a safety factor, I very often see other people as a revolver that could be pointed at me. They are the gun. I, however, am the trigger. So I speak and tread carefully. It's an effective visual aid to avoid conflicts, as I was unwittingly among people who were actually psychos underneath their dignified personas. We never know what will trigger another person's killer instinct. It can be something that happened when they were five years old. So avoid being the trigger, and the revolver will not be a threat.

This synopsis of his philosophy made such an impact on me that I immediately started reading about Carl Jung. I'm glad I did, because it helped me in my business as well as in my personal life. We are all evolving human beings, and being aware of this gave me a big boost toward maturity. It also made me less inclined to be surprised by so-called aberrant behavior. I have to stress that I am not cynical, but I am aware. I hate being in situations where I'm asking myself, How could this have happened? This reminds me of my favorite quote from Napoleon about being surprised: A good leader shouldn't be.

You have to know yourself as well as know other people to be an effective leader. For me, reading the work of Carl Jung was a step in the right direction. If someone had told me in business school that studying psychology would be important for financial success, I would not have believed it. My friend's story changed that, and I am grateful to him for such cogent advice. The relatively small number of hours I've spent reading Jung have been more than worth it. Start with his autobiography, *Memories, Dreams, Reflections*, and you will be in for a fascinating time while simultaneously fine-tuning your intuition and instincts. You will also gain a technique for seeing into—versus reading into—the people around you. Believe me, this will serve you well on many levels.

The word persona has an interesting root. It comes from the Latin word meaning mask. This, however, is not derogatory. It's necessary. Each of us has a persona. We need it for survival. It's the face we put on for public use, and it can be intentional or unconscious. For example, a salesman who has lost his entire family in an accident is, naturally, devastated. But to work effectively with his customers, he must appear cheerful and confident. That's part of his persona. It's a survival device.

The only danger is when people become their personae. That means something has been shut off somewhere along the line, and these people will end up hiding behind the false personality that works professionally. As I am very much in the public eye, this hit home and I gave it considerable thought. Fortunately, I am aware of my public side as well as my private side, and, while I'm not one for hiding much, I know there are several dimensions in which I operate. That's one reason I feel at home at The Trump Organization. The people I work with day in and day out know I'm not entirely a glam guy. They see how hard I work. One person said I am very much like a Mormon, which I took as high praise.

Anyway, reading Jung will give you insights into yourself and the ways in which you and other people operate.

Have an Ego

As you know, this rule has been easy for me to follow. But hear me out—I've got a good reason for it. Having a well-developed ego, contrary to popular opinion, is a positive attribute. It is the center of our consciousness and serves to give us a sense of purpose. I remember saying to someone, "Show me someone with no ego and I'll show you a big loser." I was trying to stir things up and provoke a reaction, but I later realized the basic idea is on target. The ego works to keep our conscious and unconscious aspects in balance. Too much either way can be detrimental. No ego means very little life force, and too much means a dictatorial personality. Keep your ego in a healthy balance, for your own well-being as well as for those around you. Strive for wholeness. It's an intelligent approach to life and business.

Understanding how egos work can be a great tool. Did you ever notice how you can deflate an opponent by simply saying, "Yeah, whatever you say. . ."? By doing this, you are gently assuming a no-ego position, which disarms the other person while at the same time taking the wind out of their sails. It gives you the peace of mind necessary to allow you to concentrate on something more important than dealing with someone who is playing God. Sometimes, rather than confronting a tyrant or a psycho directly, it's more effective to keep the knowledge to yourself and proceed accordingly, behind the scenes.

04

05

CAM

CAM

CAM

"ROSEBUD WORKS"

Errol Morris some years ago interviewed Donald Trump about Citizen Kane as part of a project called "The Movie Movie." Trump responds to the questions about his favorite film. He doesn't seem to know much about the finer grain of the film but does grasp the big picture of how the film has impacted American culture.

"The Movie Movie…was based on the idea of putting modern day figures like Trump and Mikhail Gorbachev into the movies that they most admire. So Trump would star as Kane in Citizen Kane and Gorby would be in Dr. Strangelove as who, Strangelove himself?" An interesting angle into what might be tired subjects.

Errol Morris turned the original "The Movie Movie" idea into "a four-minute clip for the 2002 Oscars of people—some of them famous: Trump, Gorbachev, Tom Brady, Christie Turlington, Keith Richards, Philip Glass, Al Sharpton—talking about their favorite movies."[86] Below is a transcript from the four-minute clip.

---

86   Kottke, Jason. "Donald Trump on Citizen Kane." Kottke.org, September 7, 2015. Web.

Morris: If you were able to give Charles Foster Kane advice, what would you say to him?

Trump: Get yourself a different woman.

Trump: [on the word Rosebud] A lot of people don't really understand the significance of it, I'm not sure if anybody understands the significance, but I think the significance is bringing a lonely, rather sad, figure back into his childhood.

Trump: The word Rosebud for whatever reason has captivated moviegoers and movie watchers for so many years and to this day, it's perhaps the single word. Perhaps if they came up with another word that meant the same thing, it wouldn't have worked. But Rosebud works.

Morris: Rosebud works.

Trump: For whatever reason.

Trump: The word Rosebud is maybe the most important word in film, and in what we all watch.

Trump: The wealth, the sorrow, the unhappiness, just struck lots of different notes.

Trump: Citizen Kane is really about accumulation. And at the end of the accumulation, you see what happened, and it's not necessarily all positive. Not positive.

Trump: I think he learned in Kane that wealth isn't anything. Because he had the wealth, but he didn't have the happiness.

Trump: [referring to well-known dinner scene in Citizen Kane] The table getting larger and larger and larger, with he and his wife getting further and further apart . . . as he got wealthier and wealthier . . . [shakes his head] perhaps I can understand that.

Trump: The relationship he had was not good for him, and probably not a great one for her, though there were benefits for her. But in the end she was not a happy camper.

Trump: In real life I do believe wealth in fact does indeed isolate you from other people . . . it's a protective mechanism. You have your guard up. Much more so then if you didn't have wealth.

Trump: That was a great rise in Citizen Kane and there was a modest fall. The fall wasn't a financial fall, the fall was a personal fall, but it was a fall nevertheless.

Trump: So you had the highs and you had the lows.

Trump: A lot of people don't understand the significance of it. I'm not sure if anybody understands the significance, but I think the significance is bringing a lonely, rather sad figure back into his childhood.

Trump: The word Rosebud for whatever reason has captivated moviegoers and movie watchers for so many years and to this day is perhaps the single word. And Perhaps if they came up with another word that meant the same thing, it wouldn't have worked. But Rosebud works.

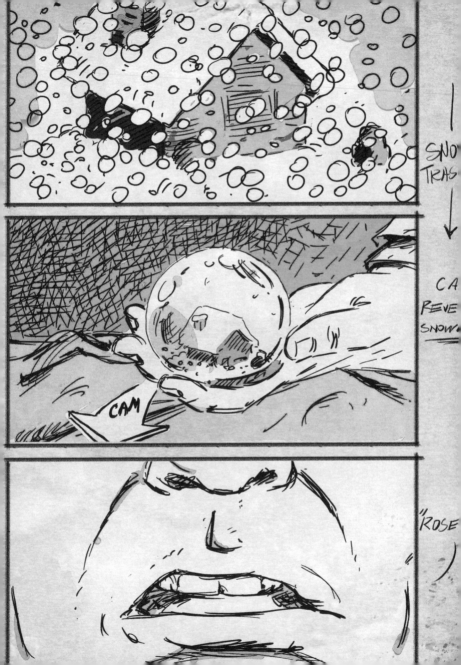

THE MASK IS
THE MESSAGE

Donald Trump is captivated by masks—not only the sort of pandemic accessory essential to daily living in 2020 (and the kind that can impact his reelection), but also the social masks of personas made famous by psychiatrist Carl Jung last century.

In his book *How to Get Rich*, Trump suggested we listen to the wisdom of Jung and learn how to shape our own personas. He also cautioned never to become your persona. What better way to perfect a persona than to practice on a TV show with audience ratings like *The Apprentice* at the height of the reality TV craze?

Noted philosopher and media guru Marshall McLuhan coined the phrase the medium is the message. He predicted ours would be a world of persona—no surprise after television merged with advertising. In the case of Donald Trump, I would suggest the man is the medium. The form is the persona or the mask.

Media critic Jean Baudrillard, who appears in *The Matrix* movie with his book *Simulacra and Simulation*, says, "All societies end up wearing masks." The question is what do the masks signify, and why do they hold an audience? If Jung were alive today, he might assign Trump the archetype of shapeshifter changing forms to confront the angry, politically correct deep state. Why is Trump so successful?

Some would attribute Trump's success to pure showmanship. Others (including this author) have likened him to Charles Foster Kane, the hard-driving, protagonist of Orson Welles' 1941 classic *Citizen Kane*. In fact, Trump himself has proclaimed the film to be his favorite. Both characters, one fictional and the other larger than life, seem to have mastered the mask.

How is it that audiences still think the show is about political bad guys and good guys but miss the scripted story behind the surface presentation? Trump created a distinctive persona. For that matter, so did Obama as community organizer. (Yes we can!) Hillary? Not so much. She came across as angry. Biden's persona is being shaped for him as the moral man with vision, but he lacks stage presence or presidential mask. A problematic reality once the stage is the thing.

Our media technology is not merely a distraction but the driving force behind the money, power, and story, all fighting to own the Matrix. Heidegger warned: "Everywhere we remain unfree and chained to technology, whether we passionately affirm or deny it. But we are delivered over to it in the worst possible way when we regard it as something neutral." Or as Jung might say, when we are no longer aware of the show.

The fatal flaw of Trump's fictional hero Citizen Kane (and like all tragic heroes, the gift that drives the hero's rise) is also the curse that causes the fall. At the end of the film, during that fall—the famous "Rosebud" scene—Kane erupts with pure anger. According to Hollywood lore, actor/director Orson Welles sliced open his hand during this scene and told others, "I really felt that." For a moment, he shed his own mask and abandoned the show.

Even with President Trump losing the election or not, will the rest of our lives be determined by the headlines on our news feeds? By a divisive media or our Amazon profiles, or more media masks? Masks can serve to introduce personas, but as Jung cautioned, we must not become the mask, or in the case of COVID-19 confuse them with the masks we wear to protect us all from disease. That's no show, that's reality.

- STUDIO
  SET UP AS OPENING

- EMPTY STUDIO

THE FORGOTTEN CITY ON A HILL

How, for the first time in American history, did a personality who lacked the credentials of political or military experience become president? Could the answer be found in the *Citizen Kane* story? Reagan, also a TV personality, viewed a Shining City on a Hill now overshadowed by global interests and stagnant wages. Before Trump's escalator descent, many in middle America had given up on the dream to work hard, save your money, and with financial growth and success, climb the social ladder. Those Obama described as people who "cling to guns or religion or antipathy to people who aren't like them" and Hillary referred to as a "basket of deplorables."

As Kane did before him with his America First campaign and wanted to be the voice to the silent majority, à la Nixon, Trump was truly tapping into the souls of the forgotten people. He was willing to play the defiant, powerful antihero descending from the heavens to stand against the dark forces working against American interest. A businessman savior who would Make American Great Again and restore that once great city. His producers from *The Apprentice* had orchestrated the grand descent. A cast of extras was hired to cheer at the event. The message he delivered would persuade the nation as did *Citizen Kane* to an American on the brink of war.

America, against the warning of its founders, was twisted in foreign entanglements and did not protect its borders or national interest. So Trump, as did Kane, delivered a potent message: Who will stand up to an establishment that exploits your wages, robs you of your dignity, and makes you live in fear? Most of the media were obsessed with uncovering Trump's bedroom vulgarity and were also tone deaf to the interests of the "flyover" people. Now Trump was promising his voters a chance to shoot down those (coastal) elitists who were flying over. Desperate or not, Trump put the world on notice: there's a new sheriff in town and he is here to Drain the Swamp and Build a Wall!

Trump's message had succeeded in forming a new posse that could fire back at the "enemy of the people." During the campaign, he had repeatedly placed a bull's-eyes on the TV outlets as "fake news." Once in office, he began sniping the press corps as they asked him loaded questions. He fired at the *New York Times* for reporting that members of special counsel Robert Mueller's team have concerns with Attorney General William

Barr's summary of its report on the Russia investigation, calling it a "fake newspaper."

But was the media's message having any effect? Was Trump's Make America Great Again strategy merely cultural nostalgia, one based on racism and cultural stubbornness? Or was it a response to a hyper-real media pushing an anti-American global vision? Reagan's City, like Trump, whether conjured by a showman or not, holds real sentiment that harkens back to Kane and his America First. Perhaps one can argue in happier times, Reagan's slogan was Let's Make America Great Again, with emphasis on the Let Us. One that implied greatness through unity and was less defensive, wrapped in the flag of E pluribus unum.

But when Trump took the stage, that trust had eroded and now he convinced many that "he alone" could do it. A rebel with a cause. He found (and also provided) the inner-city kid, the factory worker, the mothers and fathers doing the best they could. They worked hard all their lives, yet they were still falling behind. Like Kane, he knew the detached, uninvested system had ignored them completely. What makes Trump the most likeable for some Americans is the very pride in being combative and "unpredictable."

At times, it seems Trump is following a script, but at others there seems a genuine patriotism. Yes, some root for Trump to be the big dealmaker, which sounded good during the campaign, but we also need him to be our truth teller. We need him not to fall prey to the spin of dictators like Putin or Assad or Erdogan or Xi. Too often, Trump as showman appears to miss the real goals or even the clear mission. How his words, tone, and actions will impact a strategy of "getting the better of people" but put in doubt our security and future survival. And like Kane's eventual fall, what will stop Trump from turning on his own base of supporters if someday they no longer embrace his win big at-all-expense showman style?

Kane failed at his rise to governor and then returned to Xanudu, alone and rejected, but Trump is working on second term for presidency. Is there a final scene at Mar-a-Lago? Reagan had his ranch, but ranches lack borders and are open to the expanse of possibilities, to cities that burn brightly on a hill.

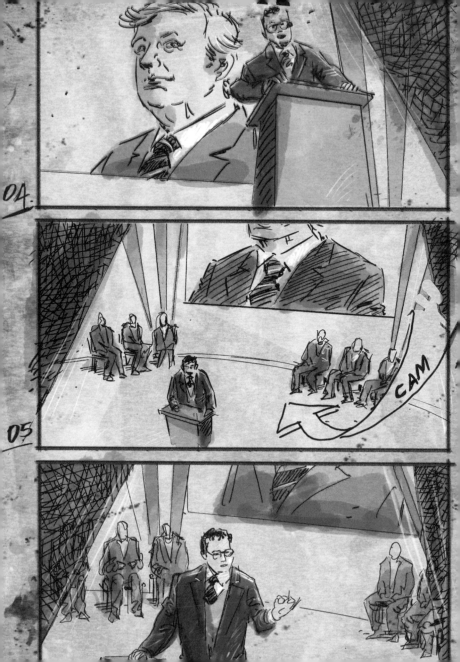

04.

05

CAM

ROSEBUD IS NOT A SLED BUT A TRAIN?

After receiving feedback on the film, I realized that my inconclusive ending regarding what Rosebud meant for Trump was not as clear as the sled in *Citizen Kane*. Though the sled was a story device, it did give an easy answer to a rather complex question.

When *Citizen Kane* first came out, Welles's own critics thought that the simple buttoned-up "Freudian" end with the sled might have been a device for simplicity, but it felt forced and might have been unnecessary for the film.

Welles had the advantage of putting the actual words "Rosebud" into the fictionalized Kane's mouth, which I did not, and it is why I chose to explore the late-night mysterious tweet covfefe as a possible final parallel.

Trump knew enough to milk the covfefe slipup, but in the end it was more revealing of his genius at playing the media than for some meaningful lost childhood symbol that he longed for most of his life.

With that written, there *is* an important childhood symbol that could offer a final parallel of Kane with Trump that is not the covfefe gag but a train set that existed in the basement of his family's Queens home.

We know from Donald Trump's childhood friend, as recently recalled in Donald's niece Mary Trump's new book, that this train set meant a lot to Donald, as did the noticeable absence of his mother, similar to the snow scene in Kane.

> From Mary Trump's book we learn "the kids spent most of their time in the basement, where the Trumps had an impressive model train set—'just splendid, trains going through tunnels and over buildings and all around,' Golding told me. 'It took up a couple ping-pong tables, a lot bigger than anything I had ever seen.' Mary Trump usually was not a part of this playtime tableau—it was Fred Trump who would come down to say hello after work. 'He was more willing to play with us, if you will, than his mom,' Golding says. 'I don't know how else to put it.'"[87]

> "Mark Golding, a close childhood friend of Trump from age six to 13, recalls being driven there by the family chauffeur. 'It had a basement that had this great electric train set up that I was really envious of Donny for having,' said Golding, 69, now a lawyer in Portland, Oregon. 'There were four or five trains and they would go all around and pass each other; one would go up a bridge and down. It was the most amazing train set you've ever seen.'"[88]

---

87   Kruse, Michael. "The Mystery of Mary Trump." *POLITICO*, November 5, 2017. Web.

88   88 Smith, David. "Donald Trump: an empire built on ego." *Taipei Times*,

Golding, the son of a physician, would sometimes sleep over. "The Trumps were among the wealthier families in Jamaica Estates. The 23-room Trump home on Midland Parkway was for some kids the cool place to go—they had a color TV, a cook, a chauffeur, an intercom system and an elaborate model train set that sticks in his class-mates' memories even half a century later. 'He had the most amazing trains,' recalled Mark Golding, a childhood friend from ages six to 13, who along with Trump attend-ed Onish's bar mitzvah. 'He had all these special gadgets and gates and switches, more extensive than anything I'd seen. I was very envious.'"[89]

Now, the timing of these stories would tie together a clear childhood symbol at a time when his mother, for rea-sons of personality or illness or otherwise, was absent from the young Donald's life.

A clear parallel to the *Citizen Kane* film.

But what we can never prove is that Trump, at one point or another in his life, voiced a word (e.g., "Lionel") in his last mo-ments before death. Maybe he will someday, maybe not.

We end this mystery with what might be a related fact, but might also just point to Trump's savvy way to self-promote.

July 20, 2016. Web.
89   Fisher, Marc. "Growing Up Trump." *Moment Magazine*, 2017. Web.

Along with board games, there is a Lionel train dedicated to Donald Trump and his presidency.[90]

---

90   "Donald Trump Legacy SD70ACE," Lionel, http://www.lionel.com/products/donald-trump-legacy-sd70ace-4545-2033430/.

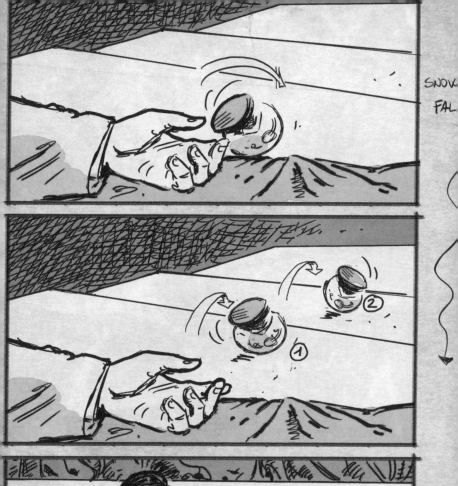

IT'S THE MEDIA, STUPID!

Trump is a Nazi. He's Hitler. He colluded with Russia. Add two impeachments, attacks from members of his own party, a non-stop fight with media, COVID-19, an insurrection, then a resurrection at CPAC…so how did Trump survive? Hint: it had nothing to do with politics—it's the media, stupid!

Nixon ignored TV and lost. Reagan mastered TV and won. Trump was Mr. Reality TV and won. His tweets became an extra line of defense. In the election against the Clinton-TV-Hollywood-media machine, Trump faced a showdown—emphasis on the show. He knew how to play the stage unlike any Republican since Reagan.

Let's face it: without COVID-19's impact on the economy, Trump had a dominant victory in November 2020. Instead, he presided over a rolling car fire, a landscape of pandemonium, lockdowns and endless summer nights of looting and vandalism by Antifa and Black Lives Matter, admittedly "trained Marxists."

Amid the chaos, even with the friendly media, Nancy Pelosi appeared a panderer to the mob. To blame capitalists was no longer a tactic, given Silicon Valley and Wall Street were on her team and determined to destroy Trump. Bezos's Washington Post aimed at the White House. CNN and MSNBC sold hatred of Trump for ratings, and unwittingly created America's lone man.

In 2016 Trump won the election, with the deplorables' revenge after they were ignored by Obama's presidency and faced with his heir apparent in Hillary Clinton. The night Trump won, the sagged faces of the media exposed bias. It was not the reaction of objective journalists, but those caught without clothes.

Trump voters had traded Ronald Reagan's city on a hill for a fight on reality TV, but TV had changed. The household male portrayed in the 1950s as Ralph Kramden, a blowhard dreamer, by the 1970s was Archie Bunker, the borderline racist, followed by Al Bundy in the 1980-1990s, a slimy sexist on Married with Children.

By the time Trump ran for office, thanks to The Shield, Dexter, and Breaking Bad, modern media had transformed white males into sociopaths. To his credit, Donald Trump never played the morality card, a strategy that blindsided Hillary and Bill Clinton. His social media was something even the deep state could not control.

He was an executive media figure with star power. What else could the voters or Nielsen ask for? He had no political experience, but he had brand recognition. From primaries to the debates, Trump lured opponents into a game show that pitted personality against politics.

In 2020, the media called Trump's reelection early, though COVID-19 had changed the process with mail-in balloting. Suspicion was warranted so Trump demanded a review of the voting process. The final straw came when he was censored by social media, left with no voice except his own megaphone on the streets of DC.

He stood against the press, high tech, and the world.

Trump's rhetoric on the streets was toxic, but no one had anticipated the audience reaction that would cross sacred lines, and hand the Democrats the one event needed to prove he was the head of a white supremacist movement. In actuality, a soft police defense was the political fallout from the BLM riots.

Without media exposure or political reinforcement, Trump could not defend the breech. Soon enough, the left grabbed all branches of government and the media battle ended. Within a DC minute, the media darling in President Biden channel-changed policies to force impeachment and mute Trump's voice.

After four years of his media rise and fall, Trump's legal team would make their final stand in a courtroom with a video montage duel—and then he reappeared at CPAC to a standing ovation. Trump would survive yet again, because though he had been blocked, he would reemerge on a media channel all his own.

Editor's note: To learn more about the book and film visit www.citizentrumpfilm.com

ACKNOWLEDGMENTS

My thanks goes to out every independent filmmaker or writer who has strove to put their original vision on a screen or on the page, however imperfectly, so that we all could better understand the world. Detailing stories and events that allow us to slip out of the distractions of media and politics and enter into an inner sanctum of common humanity. A deeper dive into character and self-understanding.

As always, thanks to my editors Anne Kimball and Erin Rodewald, who allow me to realize my thoughts during the process of writing, and rewriting, and rewriting again. Thanks to my great friends like co-filmmaker Mark Celentano and TV and sports prognosticator Bruce Rose, who were willing to read early drafts and act as my early audiences for insight and feedback. It was an honor to work again with my long term collaborator (David Orlandelli), and we're only getting started. And of course, thanks to Margo, who lives with the books, the bloviating, and beyond.

And anyone else I've missed, thank you.

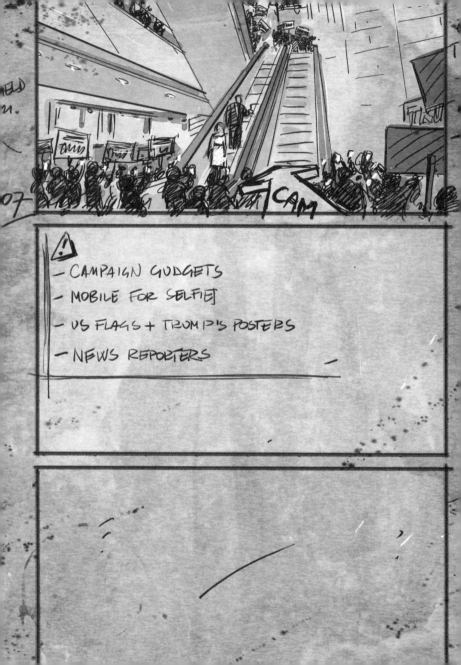

CAM

⚠️
- CAMPAIGN GUDGETS
- MOBILE FOR SELFIE
- US FLAGS + TRUMP'S POSTERS
- NEWS REPORTERS

BIBLIOGRAPHY

Anderegg, Michael. *Orson Welles, Shakespeare, and Popular Culture*. New York: Columbia University Press, 1999.

Andersen, Kurt. *Fantasyland: How America Went Haywire—A 500-Year History*. New York: Random House, 2017.

Ballantyne, T. M. *Rebuke! The Media's Failed Assault on Donald Trump*. Ballantyne Books, 2016.

Barrett, Wayne. *Trump: The Deals and the Downfall*. New York: HarperCollins, 1992.

———. *Trump: The Greatest Show on Earth—The Deals, the Downfall, the Reinvention*. New York: Regan Arts, 2016.

Bazin André, et al. *Orson Welles: A Critical View*. Acrobat Books, 1992.

Bergen, Peter. *Trump and His Generals: The Cost of Chaos*. New York: Penguin Books, 2019.

Bozell, L. Brent, and Tim Graham. *Unmasked: Big Media's War against Trump*. West Palm Beach, FL: Humanix Books, 2019.

Brady, Frank. *Citizen Welles: A Biography of Orson Welles*. London: Coronet, 1991.

Brody, David, and Scott Lamb. *The Faith of Donald J. Trump: A Spiritual Biography*. New York: Harper, an Imprint of Harper-Collins Publishers, 2018.

Brown, Michael L. *Donald Trump Is Not My Savior*. Shippensburg, PA: Destiny Image Publishers, 2018.

Callow, Simon. *Orson Welles, Volume 1: The Road to Xanadu*. New York: Viking, 1996.

———. *Orson Welles, Volume 3: One-Man Band*. New York: Viking, 2016.

Chaffetz, Jason. *The Deep State: How an Army of Bureaucrats Protected Barack Obama and Is Working to Destroy the Trump Agenda*. New York: Broadside Books, 2018.

Comey, James B. *A Higher Loyalty: Truth, Lies, and Leadership*. New York: Flatiron Books, 2019.

Corsi, Jerome R. *Killing the Deep State: The Fight to Save President Trump*. West Palm Beach, FL: Humanix Books, 2018.

Cowie, Peter. *The Cinema of Orson Welles*. Boston: Da Capo Press, 1989.

D'Antonio, Michael. *Never Enough: Donald Trump and the Pursuit of Success*. New York: Thomas Dunne Books, 2015.

Decker, Dr. *Trump's Brain: An FBI Profile of Donald Trump—Predicting Trump's Actions and Presidency*. Dr. Decker, 2018.

Farkas, Johan, and Jannick Schou. *Post-Truth, Fake News, and Democracy: Mapping the Politics of Falsehood*. New York: Routledge, 2020.

Fraser, John. *The Truth behind Trump Derangement Syndrome: There Is More than Meets the Eye*. JF Publications, 2018.

Frum, David. *Trumpocracy: The Corruption of the American Republic*. New York: Harper, 2018.

Gingrich, Newt. *Trump's America: The Truth about Our Nation's Great Comeback*. New York: Center Street, 2019.

Gordon, W. Terrence. *Everyman's McLuhan*. Mark Batty Publisher, 2007.

———. *McLuhan: A Guide for the Perplexed*. New York: Continuum, 2010.

Green, Joshua. *Devil's Bargain: Steve Bannon, Donald Trump, and the Nationalist Uprising*. New York: Penguin Books, 2018.

Gregg, Jarrett. *The Russia Hoax: The Illicit Scheme to Clear Hillary Clinton and Frame Donald Trump*. New York: Broadside Books, 2018.

Hanson, Victor Davis. *The Case for Trump*. New York, Basic Books, 2020.

Hemingway, Mollie Ziegler. *Trump vs. the Media*. New York: Encounter Books, 2017.

Higham, Charles. *Orson Welles: The Rise and Fall of an American Genius*. New York: St. Martin's Press, 1985.

Horowitz, David. *Big Agenda: President Trump's Plan to Save America*. West Palm Beach, FL: Humanix Books, 2017.

Johnston, David Cay. *It's Even Worse Than You Think: What the Trump Administration Is Doing to America*. New York: Simon & Schuster Paperbacks, 2019.

———. *The Making of Donald Trump*. Brooklyn, NY: Melville House Publishing, 2017.

Klein, Ezra. *Why We're Polarized*. New York: Avid Reader Press, 2020.

Kranish, Michael, and Marc Fisher. *Trump Revealed: An American Journey of Ambition, Ego, Money, and Power.* New York: Scribner, 2016.

Kurtz, Howard. *Media Madness: Donald Trump, the Press, and the War over the Truth.* Washington, DC: Regnery Publishing, 2018.

Leaming, Barbara. *Orson Welles: A Biography.* New York: Limelight, 1995.

Lebo, Harlan. *Citizen Kane: A Filmmaker's Journey.* New York: Thomas Dunne Books, an Imprint of St. Martin's Press, 2016.

Lee, Bandy X. *The Dangerous Case of Donald Trump: 37 Psychiatrists and Mental Health Experts Assess a President.* New York: Thomas Dunne Books, 2019.

Levin, Mark R. *Unfreedom of the Press.* New York: Threshold Editions, 2020.

Lokam, Shivaji. *The Fall of Western Civilization: How Liberalism Is Destroying the West from Within.* India: Entropy Works, LLP, 2018.

Luckovich, Mike. *"A Very Stable Genius!": @realDonaldTrump*. Toronto: ECW Press, 2018.

McKee, Robert. *Story: Substance, Structure, Style, and the Principles of Screenwriting*. New York: HarperCollins, 1997.

McLuhan, Marshall. *Understanding Media: The Extensions of Man*. Cambridge, MA: MIT Press, 1994.

McLuhan, Marshall. *The Mechanical Bride: Folklore of Industrial Man*. London: Duckworth Overlook, 2011.

McLuhan, Marshall, et al. *Essential McLuhan*. New York: Routledge, 1997.

McLuhan, Marshall, and Quentin Fiore. *The Medium Is the Massage: An Inventory of Effects*. Berkeley, CA: Gingko Press, 2017.

Merrin, William. *Baudrillard and the Media: A Critical Introduction*. Cambridge, UK: Polity Press, 2005.

Morris, Dick, and Eileen McGann. *Armageddon: How Trump Can Beat Hillary*. West Palm Beach, FL: Humanix Books, 2016.

Mueller, Robert S., and Alan M. Dershowitz. *The Mueller Report: The Final Report of the Special Counsel into Donald Trump, Russia, and Collusion*. New York: Skyhorse Publishing, 2019.

Mueller, Robert S., et al. *The Mueller Report: Presented with Related Materials by The Washington Post*. New York: Scribner, 2019.

Mulvey, Laura. *Citizen Kane*. BFI Publishing, 1992.

Naremore, James. *The Magic World of Orson Welles*. Urbana, IL: University of Illinois Press, 2015.

Nasaw, David. *The Chief: The Life of William Randolph Hearst*. Gibson Square, 2003.

O'Brien, Timothy L. *Trump Nation: The Art of Being the Donald*. New York: Warner Books, 2005.

O'Donnell, John R., and James Rutherford. *Trumped! The Inside Story of the Real Donald Trump—His Cunning Rise and Spectacular Fall*. Crossroad Press, 2018.

Poniewozik, James. *Audience of One: Donald Trump, Television, and the Fracturing of America*. New York: Liveright Publishing Corporation, 2019.

Postman, Neil. *Amusing Ourselves to Death: Public Discourse in the Age of Show Business*. New York: Penguin, 2006.

Robbins, Jeffrey W., and Clayton Crockett. *Doing Theology in the Age of Trump: A Critical Report on Christian Nationalism*. Eugene, OR: Cascade Books, 2018.

Rosenberg, Eva. *The Trump Tax Cut: Your Personal Guide to the New Tax Law*. West Palm Beach, FL: Humanix Books, 2019.

Rucker, Philip, and Carol Leonnig. *A Very Stable Genius: Donald J. Trump's Testing of America*. New York: Penguin, 2020.

Salkin, Allen, and Aaron Short. *The Method to the Madness: Donald Trump's Ascent as Told by Those Who Were Hired, Fired, Inspired—and Inaugurated*. New York: All Points Books, 2019.

Scaramucci, Anthony. *Trump: The Blue-Collar President*. New York: Center Street, Hachette Book Group, 2019.

Shapiro, Marc. *Trump This! The Life and Times of Donald Trump—An Unauthorized Biography*. Riverdale, NY: Riverdale Avenue Books, 2016.

Slater, Robert. *No Such Thing as Over-Exposure: Inside the Life and Celebrity of Donald Trump*. New York: Prentice Hall, 2017.

Stone, Roger J. *The Making of the President 2016: How Donald Trump Orchestrated a Revolution*. New York: Skyhorse Publishing, 2017.

Strauss, Barry S. *Masters of Command: Alexander, Hannibal, Caesar, and the Genius of Leadership*. New York: Simon & Schuster Paperbacks, 2013.

Swanberg, William A. *Citizen Hearst: A Biography of William Randolph Hearst*. New York: Bantam Books, 1971.

Trump, Donald J. *Crippled America: How to Make America Great Again*. New York: Threshold Editions, 2016.

Trump, Donald, and Dave Shiflett. *The America We Deserve*. Renaissance Books, 2000.

Trump, Donald J., and Meredith McIver. *Trump Never Give Up: How I Turned My Biggest Challenges into Success*. Hoboken, NJ: Wiley, 2008.

―――. *Trump Think like a Billionaire: Everything You Need to Know about Success, Real Estate, and Life*. New York: Ballantine Books, 2005.

―――. *Trump: How to Get Rich*. New York: Random House, 2004.

Trump, Donald J., and Tony Schwartz. *Trump: The Art of the Deal*. New York: Ballantine Books, 2017.

Trump, Donald J., et al. *Think Big: Make It Happen in Business and Life*. New York: Harper, 2010.

Trump, Donald J. *Great Again: How to Fix Our Crippled America*. New York: Threshold Editions, 2016.

Trump, Donald J. *Time to Get Tough: Making America Great Again!* Washington, DC: Regnery Publishing, 2015.

Trump, Ivana. *Raising Trump*. New York: Gallery Books, 2018.

Tur, Katy. *Unbelievable: My Front-Row Seat to the Craziest Campaign in American History*. New York: HarperCollins, 2017.

Vidal, Gore. *The Decline and Fall of the American Empire*. Berkeley, CA: Odonian Press, 1998.

Walsh, John Evangelist. *Walking Shadows: Orson Welles, William Randolph Hearst, and Citizen Kane*. Madison, WI: University of Wisconsin Press/Popular Press, 2004.

Welles, Orson, et al. *This Is Orson Welles*. New York: HarperCollins, 1993.

William Randolph Hearst, Orson Welles, and Citizen Kane: The History of the Men behind One of America's Most Famous Movies. Ann Arbor, MI: Charles Rivers Editors, 2019.

Wolff, Michael. *Fire and Fury: Inside the Trump White House*. New York: Henry Holt and Company, 2018.

Woodward, Bob. *Fear: Trump in the White House*. New York: Simon & Schuster, 2018.

Zimdars, Melissa, and Kembrew McLeod, eds *Fake News: Understanding Media and Misinformation in the Digital Age*. Cambridge, MA: MIT Press, 2020.

FURTHER ONLINE READING

Bailey, Jason. "What Donald Trump Didn't Learn From His Favorite Movie, 'Citizen Kane'." Flavorwire, April 28, 2016. Web.

Blum, Alexander. "Jung and the Trumpian Shadow." Quillette, October 2, 2017. Web.

Fergusson, Patsy. "Trump Is America's Jungian Shadow." Medium. Fourth Wave, August 22, 2020. Web.

Hufbauer, Benjamin. "How Trump's Favorite Movie Explains Him." POLITICO Magazine, June 6, 2016. Web.

Kottke, Jason. "Donald Trump is modeling his life after Charles Foster Kane." Kottke.org, October 26, 2016. Web.

Phillips, Michael. "Is Donald Trump Charles Foster Kane in Disguise?" Chicago Tribune, August 26, 2015. Web.

Shapiro, Alan N. "Orwell, Baudrillard and Trump." Alan N. Shapiro, Autonomy in the Digital Society, February 19, 2017. Web.

Willmore, Alison. "How Donald Trump Totally Missed The Point Of 'Citizen Kane' - And Won." BuzzFeed, November 11, 2016. Web.